DEATH IN THE NURSERY

Death in the Nursery

The Secret Crime of Infanticide

James Manney and John C. Blattner

SERVANT BOOKS
Ann Arbor, Michigan

Published by Servant Books
P.O. Box 8617
Ann Arbor, Michigan 48107

Cover illustration © 1984 by David Hile
Book design by John B. Leidy

Printed in the United States of America
ISBN 0-89283-192-8

Library of Congress Cataloging in Publication Data

Manney, James D.
  Death in the nursery.

  Includes index.
  1. Neonatal intensive care—Moral and ethical aspects.
2. Infanticide—Moral and ethical aspects. 3. Infants
(Newborn)—Legal status, laws, etc. 4. Medical ethics.
I. Blattner, John. II. Title.
RJ253.5.M36 1984   174′.24   84-13930
ISBN 0-89283-192-8

For the Children

Contents

Acknowledgments

WE RECEIVED THE GENEROUS HELP of many men and women during the months we researched and wrote this book.

C. Everett Koop, M.D., the Surgeon General of the United States, has been concerned with the treatment of handicapped newborns for many years. He, more than anyone else, is responsible for bringing the issue of infanticide to public attention and for the progress that has been made in protecting the civil rights of handicapped newborns. Dr. Koop took time out from his busy schedule to meet with us and to give us guidance on both the medical and governmental aspects of infanticide.

Stephen Galebach, deputy director of the White House office of legal policy, was instrumental in pointing us toward this topic and provided invaluable guidance along the way. We benefitted greatly from his help and from the hospitality provided by him and his wife, Diane. We are glad to have such gracious friends.

James Bopp, Jr., general counsel of the National Right to Life Committee, and Thomas Marzen, chief staff counsel of the Americans United for Life Legal Defense Fund, helped us understand the Infant Doe case and the legal aspects of infanticide.

Evan Kemp, Jr., director of the Disability Rights Center, is a skillful advocate for handicapped people who helped us see the connection between the problems of handicapped newborns and prejudice against disabled people generally.

We also profited greatly from our discussions with Paul Marchand, director of the Washington office of the Association for Retarded Citizens. Along with Dr. Koop, he continues to play a key role in the effort to provide civil rights protection for handicapped newborns.

The research for this book was made much easier than it otherwise would have been because Dr. Joseph Stanton, M.D., made his files available to us. He is a wise and generous physician who has inspired many by his defense of the sanctity of life.

We were glad to be able to spend time with Carl and Rachel Rossow and their children. We count ourselves among the many who have been inspired by the heroic example of the Rossow family.

Others who helped us include Steven Baer and Burke Balch of Americans United for Life; Douglas Badger of the Christian Action Council; Janet Carroll and Douglas Johnson of the National Right to Life Committee; Gary Curran of the American Life Lobby; Melinda Delahoyde, author and advocate for handicapped infants; Congressmen John Erlenborn and Henry Hyde and their staffs; Orzie Henderson, M.D.; Carl Horn, formerly of the Civil Rights Division of the Justice Department; Thomas Nearney of the office of Special Education and Rehabilitative Services of the U.S. Department of Education; Rebecca Patrias, M.D.; and Carlton Sherwood of the Washington *Times*.

Special thanks to Stephen Peterson, president and publisher of Servant Publications, for Servant's early and strong support.

Writing a book tends to absorb every available hour, as our wives, Sue Manney and Peggy Blattner, now know very well. They not only tolerated this project but encouraged and helped us. Our thanks to them.

These people, and a few who go unnamed, deserve credit for the book's strengths. We are responsible for its defects.

—James Manney and John C. Blattner

Part I

The Secret Crime

ONE

The Untold Story of Infant Doe

"The baby was killed because it was retarded."
—George F. Will

INFANT DOE WAS BORN on Good Friday, April 9, 1982. He died miserably six days later of starvation and dehydration in a hospital room, his body shrunken, blood running from a mouth too dry to close.

Doctors and nurses in the hospital could have fed the starving boy. But his parents forbade food and water, and a court order backed them up.

Consternation over Infant Doe's plight had spread far beyond Bloomington Hospital in Bloomington, Indiana.

At the moment of Infant Doe's death, two lawyers were boarding a plane to Washington to make a desperate appeal for his life before Justice John Paul Stevens of the U.S. Supreme Court. The day before the baby's death, President Ronald Reagan had asked the Justice Department and the Department of Health and Human Services to find a way for the federal government to intervene.

All their efforts failed. Infant Doe died because his parents desired his death, a doctor issued the orders to bring it about, and two Indiana courts sanctioned it.

Why? Because Infant Doe was one of perhaps ten babies born in the United States on April 9 with Down's syndrome, a chromosomal defect that usually causes a mild form of mental retardation.

The *Washington Post* observed: "The Indiana baby died, not because he couldn't sustain life without a million dollars worth of medical machinery, but because no one fed him."

Syndicated columnist George Will put it more bluntly: "The baby was killed because it was retarded."

The torrent of outrage that erupted when Infant Doe died has made him a symbol of infanticide. His legacy lives on. His death led directly to federal regulations and congressional legislation aimed at stopping such killings in the future. But stopping them will not be easy. Infant Doe's death focused public attention on an alarming fact—that "nontreatment" of unwanted handicapped infants happens in American hospitals.

Outrage over this baby's fate is appropriate. There is much to be outraged about in the brief life and squalid death of Infant Doe.

Little information about Infant Doe's parents is on the public record. Jerry Bales, an Indiana state representative from Bloomington, calls them "the salt of the earth. The nicest people you ever want to meet."[1] They are professional people, college-educated, parents of two other children. The father is a public school teacher. He told a court that he has worked with Down's syndrome children on occasion and that "he and his wife felt that a minimally acceptable quality of life was never present for a child suffering from such a condition."[2]

It is sometimes said that handicapped infants should be eased into death because caring for them will be too expensive. From what we know of Infant Doe's parents, it is not unreasonable to assume that they had adequate insurance to cover a lengthy hospital stay. It is also possible that they could have afforded good medical care, high quality education, and other resources that would have made life with a mentally impaired child easier. They were, in fact, able to hire a very good private attorney. Their obstetrician, Dr. Walter L. Owens, happens to be one of the busiest physicians in Bloomington.

Very soon after Dr. Owens delivered Infant Doe in Bloomington Hospital at 8:19 P.M. on April 9, the decision was made to let the six-pound baby die.

We will probably never fully know how the parents reached this decision, but a few things are clear about it.

Dr. Owens readily supported the decision and participated in it. He holds mentally impaired people in low regard: he later testified that "some of these [Down's syndrome] children are mere blobs."[3]

The parents were quite definite in their decision. They refused the advice of other doctors who insisted that their son be treated, and went to great lengths to make sure he died. Their expenses included the fees of an attorney to represent them in court, the cost of a private hospital room for their baby to die in, and the cost of a private nurse to stand watch.

Finally, their decision was made in haste and in considerable ignorance. Andrew Mallor, the parents' attorney, told the court and the press that the baby would have been "severely retarded." If Infant Doe's parents believed that, they were misled. The degree of retardation in a Down's child cannot be known for years, and most people with this condition are only mildly retarded.

In other words, it was almost certainly prejudice against the handicapped—dislike of "mongoloids" and fear at having given birth to a "monster"—that led to the death sentence for Infant Doe.

None of this was immediately known to Dr. James Schaffer and Dr. James Laughlin, two pediatricians who were summoned to examine Infant Doe the night he was born. They could see that the infant almost certainly had Down's syndrome. A visual diagnosis can usually be made by looking at the baby's face. Infant Doe had the flat face and short nose characteristic of Down's.

X-rays ordered by the doctors showed that the baby had serious problems—life-threatening problems. Infant Doe had a defective digestive system—esophageal atresia with tracheo-esophageal fistula. The atresia was an open esophagus; if fed normally, he would vomit, and food would flow into his lungs. The fistula was an opening that would allow gastric juices to flow into the lungs. Either way, the baby would get pneumonia.

It was not surprising that Infant Doe's life was in danger. Many Down's babies are born with serious clinical problems, usually an abnormal digestive system like Infant Doe's or congenital heart problems.

Dr. Schaffer and Dr. Laughlin were immediately concerned about the life-threatening atresia and fistula. They recommended surgery. In fact, Infant Doe stood a very good chance of coming through surgery in good shape. Later in the drama it would be claimed that the surgery carried high risks, that it would have been difficult, that Infant Doe was too sick to go on the operating table. All of these statements are false. According to Dr. James Laughlin he had well over a 90 percent chance of doing well.[4]

The crucial fact is that no one would have dreamed of refusing such surgery for a baby who did not have Down's syndrome.

The consulting pediatricians gave their recommendation to Infant Doe's parents: he should have immediate surgery to repair the fistula and atresia. Because Bloomington Hospital was not equipped for the operation, the boy should be flown to Riley Hospital for Children in Indianapolis, sixty miles away.

They were stunned when the parents refused. "John and Mary Doe" had already discussed the matter with Dr. Owens and had decided their son would be better off dead. They were not going to have the baby fed intravenously. Dr. Owens had already issued the orders to the nurses. Infant Doe was going to starve to death in Bloomington Hospital while the staff who could save him stood by helplessly.

These things happen in American hospitals. In most cases no one outside the hospital finds out about them. Nurses are afraid to speak out. Doctors, as we shall see in later chapters, are not unsympathetic to parents who do not want to raise handicapped children. Doctors also are loathe to second-guess each other, and they dislike a court or a government agency getting involved in clinical treatment decisions.

But the Infant Doe case took a different turn. Fury erupted on the staff. Physicians strenuously protested the case to hospital administrators. Nurses were incensed. Said one nurse, "Who do they think they are—asking me to help them commit infanticide?"[5]

There was, hospital administrator Roland Kohr said, "violent disagreement" on the hospital staff about what to do about Infant Doe.[6]

Even so, administrators did nothing to intervene. They did not review the case, convene a committee of physicians to look into it, or do anything else to halt the starvation occurring in the nursery.

Yet the hospital was vulnerable. Dr. Owens was an obstetrician; by ordering nourishment withheld from Infant Doe, he was practicing pediatrics. The hospital's pediatricians strenuously opposed Dr. Owens' "treatment" for the baby.

In other words, Infant Doe was not Dr. Owens's patient. If administrators allowed Dr. Owens to continue, they would be permitting a violation of the hospital's own rules.

Facing a bitter conflict among doctors, a rebellion on the nursing staff, resolute parents, and an irregular internal situation, the hospital administrators decided to go to court.

On Saturday, April 10, hospital attorney Len Bunger called Judge John Baker of the Monroe County Circuit court and filled him in on the unfolding drama at Bloomington Hospital. Baker was well known to hospital administrators. His wife was a vice president of the Local Council of Women, which owned the hospital. Another relative was a member of the hospital's board of directors. Bunger explained the hospital's problem.

That evening, Judge Baker held an emergency hearing in a conference room on the hospital's sixth floor and heard testimony from all parties present—Drs. Owens, Schaffer, and Laughlin, the baby's father, and hospital administrators.

One party, however, was not represented—Infant Doe.

He should have been. Indiana juvenile law requires that the court appoint a guardian to represent the child's interests in a hearing on a charge of child neglect. The legal term is *guardian ad litem*. The guardian's job is to argue for the child. Judge Baker, however, did not appoint a guardian that night. He never explained why he did not but merely commented that he was watching out for Infant Doe's interests himself.

Did Judge Baker's action—more accurately, his inaction—on the guardian matter violate Indiana juvenile law? Some think the Judge erred by not appointing a guardian Saturday night. It was at least highly irregular. If judges can adequately represent the interests of children and infants in child neglect hearings, why should the state have a law requiring the appointment of guardians?

That night, Judge Baker gave an oral decision. He issued a written opinion two days later, on Monday. He gave Dr. Owens and Infant Doe's parents everything they wanted. The Judge said the legal issue was simply whether the parents had the right to make the decision they did. They were faced with conflicting medical options, the Judge said, treatment or nontreatment. They were within their rights to chose the latter. In the Judge's view, refusal of low-risk life-sustaining surgery and withdrawal of food and water constituted a "treatment." As Judge Baker put it in his written opinion, the parents "have the right to choose a medically recommended course of treatment for their child in the present circumstances."[7]

Judge Baker's decision got the hospital off the hook. He directed the hospital to carry out obstetrician Dr. Owens's orders for pediatric patient Infant Doe.

On Monday the Judge belatedly appointed a guardian for the starving baby—the county's welfare department. He said he did this to force an appeal of his ruling. It didn't work out that way. The department's child protection team met that day, discussed the case, and decided to stay out of it.

On Tuesday, Judge Baker named Bloomington attorney Phil Hill, husband of a juvenile court referee, to be the new guardian.

The case of Infant Doe appeared to be as good as closed. Only the hospital staff and a handful of people in Bloomington's legal community knew about the starvation occurring in the hospital nursery.

But Phil Hill was troubled. He didn't like what was going on. He gave the case its next fateful twist.

Phil Hill picked up the phone and called Barry Brown, Monroe County Prosecutor.

Brown had every reason to stay away from the case. He was a politician. No one was demanding that he act. If he did, some powerful people in Bloomington would be very unhappy. Sympathy seemed to lie with the parents of a child people were calling "severely retarded." What would be gained if the prosecutor dragged parents, doctors, and hospital into court?

But Brown thought he might be able to save Infant Doe's life.On Tuesday, April 13, Brown asked the Monroe Juvenile Court for an emergency order to remove Infant Doe from his parents' custody and provide him with medical care until a court could determine whether he was a victim of child neglect. Infant Doe had not been fed for four days. It was imperative to act *now*, he said.

That afternoon, Juvenile Judge Pro-Tem Thomas Spencer

held another hearing, reviewed the evidence, and turned down Brown's emergency request. He agreed with Judge Baker that the issue was whether the parents had acted responsibly. Since they had consulted physicians at length, they were not guilty of neglect. For Spencer as well as Baker, nontreatment was a form of treatment.

A bitterly disappointed Barry Brown would not give up. He decided to take one more step to save the baby's life—an emergency appeal to the Indiana State Supreme Court in Indianapolis. Brown secured the court's permission to hold an emergency hearing the next afternoon. Brown and Deputy Prosecutor Larry Brodeur stayed up all night preparing their case.

Infant Doe was five days old on the morning of the State Supreme Court hearing. Not a word about the flurry of medical and legal activity over his plight had yet appeared in the press. Court proceedings regarding juveniles are closed to the press and public. Reporters on the court beat for the Bloomington *Herald-Telephone* knew nothing about Judge Baker's and Judge Spencer's hearings, nor were they likely to. Juvenile Court records are customarily sealed.

But the drama of the past five days—the death sentence, the participation of doctors, the sanction of the courts—was about to become public.

To schedule the emergency appeal in the Infant Doe case, the State Supreme Court had preempted a previously scheduled hearing in a criminal case that the Indianapolis press had been following. But word of the schedule change didn't get through to the press. Thus, reporters were sitting in the courtroom when Brown, Brodeur, and Hill began to plead for the life of a Down's syndrome infant being starved to death in Bloomington Hospital because his parents didn't want him.

The news flashed across the country immediately.

The Bloomington attorneys asked the State Supreme Court to order the lower court to declare that the child was covered under the state's Child in Need of Services law, a step which would assure that he would be fed intravenously. It was truly an emergency motion. To do what Brown and the others asked, the State Supreme Court would have to hold that the lower courts had clearly failed to do their duty. Hill and the prosecutors based their highly unusual request on the claim that Infant Doe's right to life superseded the parental rights that Judges Baker and Spencer had found so compelling.

Brodeur urged the justices to act immediately. "The child," he said, "is at this very moment at Bloomington Hospital starving to death."

The court turned him down. Late Wednesday afternoon, the justices voted three to one not to intervene. No written opinion was issued.

One curious detail in this proceeding was noted by some of the reporters who rushed to report the decision: Chief Justice Richard Givan had not been present in court to hear the appeal, yet he voted with the majority to deny it.[8]

Givan aggressively defended the court's decision. He told the *Indianapolis Star* that the baby was too sick to survive surgery and that he had an abnormal heart.[9] The autopsy on Infant Doe and other medical evidence showed both claims to be false.

On April 16, Chief Justice Givan sealed all legal records in the case. They have remained sealed ever since.

Infant Doe had little more than twenty-four hours to live by the time his plight became public. The legal defense of his right to life had just about run its course, but other efforts to save him intensified.

At least ten couples came forward and offered to adopt the child, according to Barry Brown. The most determined among these were Bobby and Shirley Wright of Evansville, parents of a three-year-old daughter with Down's syndrome. They wanted to add Infant Doe to their family. To press their case, they retained James Bopp, Jr., a Terre Haute attorney who is general counsel for the National Right to Life Committee.

On Thursday, only hours before Infant Doe's death, Bopp went before Judge Baker and argued that the baby should be kept alive so the Wrights could adopt him. Infant Doe's parents were neglecting him, he said. Through their attorney, "John and Mary Doe" argued vehemently against allowing their son to be adopted.

Judge Baker turned the Wrights down. Since Infant Doe's parents were following a "course of treatment" recommended by Dr. Owens, they were not neglecting him nor had they abandoned him.[10] Therefore, the court need not entertain the idea that he needed adoptive parents.

Fumed Bopp: "The treatment is no treatment. It's *1984*. It's Newspeak. It's 'peace is war.'"

As the news spread, bewildered and angry citizens wrote to the newspapers and called Bloomington Hospital. Picketers protesting the starvation appeared outside the hospital. One carried a sign calling Bloomington Hospital "the new death camp." Television crews descended on Bloomington and reporters pieced together the events of the past week.

The final event that assured that Infant Doe will never be forgotten occurred at some point on Thursday.

President Ronald Reagan learned about what was going on in Bloomington Hospital. He acted swiftly, telling the Department of Health and Human Services and the Justice Department to find a way to intervene.

Infant Doe died before federal officials could help, but the President's interest did not weaken. Infant Doe's death led directly to the "Baby Doe regulations," which attempted to use federal regulatory power to protect the civil rights of handicapped infants. The rules brought disability rights and prolife groups into a coalition and pitted them in a struggle with powerful elements of organized medicine that threatens to continue through the 1980s and beyond.

Barry Brown and Larry Brodeur decided to try one last legal

remedy—an appeal to Justice John Paul Stevens, the U.S. Supreme Court Justice responsible for the courts in Indiana. Brodeur and Patrick Baude, a professor of constitutional law at Indiana University, boarded a plane at Indianapolis International airport for Washington via Atlanta at 10:10 P.M.

After they landed in Atlanta, Brodeur called Brown from a pay phone in the Delta Airlines Terminal. Brown told him the sad news: Infant Doe had died at 10:03 P.M., seven minutes before they had left Indianapolis. Brodeur and Baude returned to Bloomington.

Infant Doe was dying this Thursday night while the President of the United States, two cabinet departments, and numerous people in Bloomington tried to devise a way to save him. Because of the hostility of the hospital staff and the growing controversy, his parents had moved him to a private room and hired a private nurse to stand watch. He cried almost continuously as he starved. Toward the end, however, he grew silent. He developed pneumonia. His tiny body shrank pitifully as he grew more dehydrated. Blood oozed from his dry, cracked mouth, discoloring the clean hospital sheet under his head.

Pediatrician Dr. James Schaffer had agitated throughout the week to save Infant Doe. Thursday morning he decided he had had enough. He went to the infant's room with intravenous feeding equipment, prepared to attach the tubes. But it was too late for Infant Doe. "Too late for fluids, too late for surgery, too late for justice," commented Dr. Ann Bannon, a pediatrician who studied the case.[11]

Everyone had failed him—his parents, doctors, the hospital, the courts.

His parents did do one thing for him. Later, when they faced accusations of child neglect, John and Mary Doe instructed their attorney to tell the press how they had cared for their son. One of the things they did, Attorney Mallor said, was to have Infant Doe baptized before he died.[12] Fr. Robert F. Borchertmeyer of St. Charles Borromeo parish in Bloomington baptized him a Roman Catholic on April 12.[13]

Controversy and recrimination erupted immediately after Infant Doe's death.

"If there is a law, I wish someone would point it out to me," Judge Baker told the press the day after the baby died.[14]

Brown and Brodeur thought about filing criminal charges, but decided against it. "The parents and physician," he said, "were proceeding under the color of law."[15]

What law? many asked. "If starving a baby to death is not neglect, then what the hell is?" asked Nat Hentoff in *The Village Voice*.

Others were similarly appalled.

"In at least one state it is now permissible to do to a retarded, deformed infant what would be illegal if done to a dog or cat," wrote columnist Stephan Chapman in the *Chicago Tribune*.

Said Joseph Sobran on CBS radio: "I used to think my fellow abortion foes were a little hysterical for predicting that this sort of thing was just around the corner. We now have concrete evidence that they were right: civilization is on a slippery slope, and barbarisms that were once universally condemned are now gaining acceptance as normal behavior."

Wrote the editor of *The Virginian-Pilot*, "How good can life possibly be in a society that yawns—or worse, applauds—when courts order physicians not to treat a helpless infant?"

Columnist George Will wrote perhaps the most pointed and poignant comment on the case. He wrote about his son Jonathan, then ten, who has Down's syndrome. Jonathan "does not 'suffer from' Down's syndrome," Will wrote. "He is the best whiffle-ball hitter in Southern Maryland and suffers only from anxiety about the Baltimore Orioles' lousy start.

"He is doing nicely, thank you. But he is bound to have enough problems dealing with society—receiving rights, let alone empathy. He can do without people like Infant Doe's parents and courts like Indiana's asserting that people like him are less than fully human. On the evidence, Down's syndrome citizens have little to learn about being human from the people responsible for the death of Infant Doe."

Infant Doe was not forgotten. Larry Brodeur took over from Phil Hill as the baby's *guardian ad litem*, and he tenaciously pursued the case through the courts. Chief Justice Richard Givan had sealed court records the day after the baby's death. In a succession of appeals and motions, assisted by the Americans United for Life Legal Defense Fund, Brodeur attempted to get the records unsealed. He failed, even though he argued that the legal issues were of compelling public interest and volunteered to keep the identity of the baby's parents secret. A final appeal to the U.S. Supreme Court was turned down in November 1983.

But the legacy of Infant Doe was assured on April 30, 1982, scarcely two weeks after the baby's death, when President Ronald Reagan ordered the Department of Health and Human Services to notify hospitals that infanticide would not be permitted. The Department's Office for Civil Rights issued the notice on May 18. Under federal law, it told 6,450 hospital administrators, it is unlawful "to withhold from a handicapped infant nutritional sustenance or medical or surgical treatment required to correct a life-threatening condition."

The death of Infant Doe lifted the veil covering the secret crime.

TWO

The Secret Crime

"The average American would be shocked at the decisions that are made regarding 'non-perfect' infants."
—Nurse in Kentucky

T HE MONROE COUNTY CORONER, Dr. John Pless, ruled that Infant Doe died of "natural causes." The baby's death, however, was a case of infanticide. His case was exceptional only in the attention it attracted. Parents and their agents have been putting unwanted babies to death for centuries. They are still doing it in American hospitals.

Historically, parents have taken care of this gruesome business themselves.

Eskimos and other peoples living on the edge of survival have often disposed of babies with physical defects by exposing them to the elements. In Chinese and other cultures, a strong bias in favor of male children often led to the killing of unwanted female babies. In medieval Europe, unmarried mothers often disposed of their babies to hide the evidence of their sin.

Parents still take these matters into their own hands.

Baby Boy McKay died on June 28, 1983, thirty-nine minutes after he was born in Ingalls Memorial Hospital in Harvey, Illinois. The boy was born with a cleft palate and a clenched fist—two visible deformities that are nonetheless correctable. But Daniel McKay, the boy's father who was present in the delivery room, went into a rage when he saw the child. When the physician turned aside for a moment, Daniel allegedly smashed his son's head on the delivery room floor two times, killing him.

Daniel McKay was beloved by his neighbors in a small Illinois town. He was a veternarian. He would often stay up at night to save the life of a sick pet.[1]

Susan and Ted killed their baby at home. Susan and Ted live somewhere in Connecticut; they spoke anonymously to a reporter from the *Hartford Courant*. Without revealing many details about their child, even its sex, Susan and Ted told the reporter that their child came home from the hospital very sick and in need of constant care. They had to feed it through a tube and also administer anti-convulsive medicine to control seizures.

After a few weeks, Susan and Ted began to increase the amount of medicine administered by eyedropper into the feeding tube. On the sixth day after they began, the baby died. The parents talked to a doctor friend before the final, fatal sedation. The doctor approved their action. "Their baby was essentially socially dead," he said.[2]

In the U.S. today, infanticide usually happens in hospitals. Handicapped babies are occasionally killed by a direct act but more often the deed is done by withholding something the infant needs to survive. Sometimes food and water are withheld. Sometimes the baby will not get an operation it needs in order to survive, an operation a "normal" baby would always receive. Doctors sometimes sedate babies with large doses of drugs so that they will starve quietly without crying for food. Sometimes antibiotics are withheld so that the baby will die of infection. Sometimes the "plug" is pulled on a life-support system because someone has decided that the struggling infant will not have an adequate "quality of life."

"The average American would be shocked at the decisions

that are made regarding 'non-perfect' infants," a nurse in Lexington, Kentucky, wrote to a federal agency. "I have personally heard physicians and nurses talk to new parents about their child and persuade the parents to 'let the child die and therefore end its suffering'—which really meant 'let us starve your child to death.' "[3]

Many Americans were shocked when two eminent pediatricians published an article in 1973 in a prestigious medical journal detailing a pattern of what can only be called infanticide in the intensive care nursery at Yale-New Haven Hospital, one of the nation's great medical centers. Dr. Raymond S. Duff and Dr. A.G.M. Campbell studied 299 deaths that had occurred in the nursery over an eighteen month period. Forty-three deaths—14 percent of the total— had been caused by medical personnel withholding or withdrawing treatment.

Duff and Campbell claimed that they were merely breaking the silence about a common practice in hospital nurseries. They concluded with a chilling challenge: "If working out these dilemmas in ways such as those we suggest is in violation of the law, we believe the law should be changed."[4]

Among those protesting the Duff-Campbell policies were Dr. Joan Venes and Dr. Peter Huttenlocher of Yale Medical School. But in dissociating themselves from their eminent colleagues, they confirmed the existence of the problem. "It is troubling to us," they wrote in the *New England Journal of Medicine*, "to hear young pediatric interns ask first 'should we treat?' rather than 'how do we treat?' "[5]

This is the question people asked about the "The Hopkins Baby" in 1970 at Johns Hopkins Medical Center in Baltimore. Like Infant Doe, the boy was born with Down's Syndrome and a defective intestine that needed surgical repair if he was to eat normally. One of the doctors recommended the surgery and spoke up for Down's victims. Down's syndrome, he told the boy's parents, "is one of the milder forms of mental retardation. . . . They're almost always trainable. They can hold simple jobs. And they're famous for being happy children. They're perenially happy and usually a great joy."[6]

But the parents did not want their son to live and doctors in the hospital's newborn nursery cooperated with them. The parents refused surgery and ordered that the baby not be fed. One doctor on the unit spoke of how uncomfortable he was talking to the parents on the phone during the fifteen days it took the child to die. "They would ask how things were going," he said, "and I had to tell them 'fine, just fine. It's just taking a little longer than we thought.'"

One other thing made the death of the Hopkins baby especially significant.

It was done openly. The decision was not a squalid and secret deed. A movie was made about the death of the Hopkins Baby. Some of the physicians and nurses who participated in the original case portrayed themselves in the dramatic re-creation. The purpose of the film was to deplore what had happened, but Dr. C. Everett Koop, U.S. Surgeon-General, says that the film is now shown in some medical schools to train students in the proper management of a difficult pediatric case.

These are some of the events that brought infanticide out in the open. However, the press, which grew in aggressiveness and prestige during these post-Watergate years, was curiously silent.

A reporter for the Gannett chain named Carlton Sherwood came across the Duff article and the Hopkins film in 1979 and wrote about infanticide. His editor killed the story. A year later, after winning a Pulitizer Prize, Sherwood tried again. His editor killed the story once more, insisting that no one would be interested.

Sherwood says that medical editors do not like stories that reflect negatively on medical professionals. He also thinks that even good reporters "abandon their normal skepticism" when talking to physicians. They tend to report what doctors say without further checking.

Sherwood finally did his infanticide story in 1983 as an investigative reporter for WNEV-TV in Boston. He interviewed parents, interrogated physicians, and reviewed medical records. His film series made a powerful case that infanticide is becoming a widespread practice accepted in American hospitals.

Another reporter who followed the story was Diane Brozek of the *Hartford Courant*. In 1981, eight years after the Duff-Campbell article appeared, she investigated practices at Yale-New Haven. Her conclusion: "At the intensive care nursery at Yale-New Haven hospital...sometimes life-saving medicine or surgery is withheld. Other infants are allowed to starve to death. And in some cases, doctors at Yale-New Haven have helped parents give their defective infants lethal drug overdoses."[7]

Exposure of another sort came from Dr. Koop. He wrote about infanticide in *Whatever Happened to the Human Race?*, a book he co-authored with theologian Francis A. Schaeffer. The book was widely read by Christians and prolife activists, and a movie based on it gained wide exposure. This was not the sort of audience to make the media elite sit up and take note, but it helped galvanize the prolife movement and set the stage for the uproar that followed the death of Infant Doe.

We must be clear about what infanticide is *not*. Not every decision to withhold or withdraw treatment from a gravely ill infant can be called infanticide.

It is not good medicine to pointlessly prolong the life of a baby who is born dying. If the best medical judgment holds that an infant will live only a short time after birth, doctors need not attach it to a respirator, perform an operation, or launch other involved treatments that would merely delay imminent death for a brief time.

Neither is it infanticide to withdraw a useless treatment. If, for example, the best medical judgment is that a treatment is doing a patient no good, then that treatment need not be continued even if withdrawing it means that the individual will die. Treatments should be continued only if they are *medically* effective. The point, of course, is that this is a *medical* decision, not one based on social convenience or estimates of the quality of someone's future life.

Nor is it infanticide to refuse "extraordinary" means to sustain life. Barney Clark was not morally obligated to let surgeons give him an artificial heart. Parents do not have to authorize an operation with a small chance of success or an experimental therapy whose effects are unknown. They do not have to keep their child alive for purposes of medical research.

The idea of extraordinary means has been much abused. Infanticide has often been committed by people who conveniently call ordinary treatments "extraordinary." But the concept is very simple, much simpler than the advocates of infanticide-on-demand are willing to admit. The difference between ordinary and extraordinary treatments is this: if the treatment considered for a handicapped infant is one that would be given without question to a "normal" baby, it is an "ordinary" treatment. The handicapped baby should receive it. If the treatment would be heroic and extraordinary for the "normal" baby, it can reasonably be withheld from the handicapped child. The handicap—mental retardation, crippled limbs, incontinent bladder—should not determine whether the newborn will be allowed to live.

In fact, this distinction is one of the best ways to identify infanticide. Babies who are targets for infanticide are unwanted for *non-medical* reasons. Their care will be expensive. They have survived an abortion. They will never walk. They will be burdens to parents and siblings. They will lead "unproductive" lives. They might end up in an institution at state expense. Above all, children in the United States are likely to be unwanted if they will suffer some degree of mental impairment. When such children need something to keep them alive—a routine operation, antibiotic therapy, even food and water—they may not get it in American hospitals today.

Says a mother in Montana: "My daughter Keough was born in November 1980 with Down's syndrome and a host of other defects in her digestive system similar to Baby Doe's problems. Twenty minutes after her birth our then pediatrician offered to let her starve in the hospital nursery."

A Texas physician: "The 'very strict standard' [requiring treatment for handicapped infants] is probably close to *uniformly not* being followed" in the medical community.

The Association for Retarded Citizens: "Our members can cite numerous examples of improper and wrong advice given to them by physicians about the future capacities of their children."[8]

Which children become targets for infanticide?

Perhaps the most frequent targets are those children born with Down's syndrome. Their disability is one of the most common birth defects, occurring once in every 600-1,000 births. A large number of Down's infants are also born with life-threatening medical problems, such as heart defects and malformed digestive systems, which require prompt and effective care. They often do not receive this care because their particular disability—mental retardation—is despised in a society that prizes intelligence above all else.

Down's syndrome was Phillip Becker's problem. Although the mental impairment that results from it is not fatal, it almost cost Phillip his life.

In 1980, the medical consultants at the state home where Phillip lived in California decided that the cheerful thirteen-year-old boy needed an operation to correct a heart defect. Without it, he would die slowly and painfully over a number of years. But Phillip's parents, who had institutionalized him at birth, refused to consent to the surgery

Two California courts went along with the Beckers, even though Phillip's father admitted that he would not hesitate to order such an operation on one of his mentally normal sons.

Two years later, however, another California judge gave this story a happy ending. He found that the Beckers' treatment of Phillip constituted neglect and he allowed another couple to adopt Phillip. Pat and Herb Heath, his new parents, had the heart operation performed in 1983. It appears to have been a complete success.[9]

Another category of infants at risk are those with spina bifida. This condition consists of a lesion, or hole, in the spinal column which causes physical disability. Most spina bifida victims do not walk normally. Many are confined to wheelchairs, and some have incontinent bladders, for the rest of their lives. For two reasons, rapid and effective treatment is usually essential for a spina bifida newborn. Surgery to close the hole in the spine is needed to prevent further loss of function. Also, many spina bifida children need a shunt implanted to drain excess fluid from their brain. If neglected, many such children will die, and those who survive will be very severely disabled.

Baby Jane Doe was born with spina bifida in a Long Island, New York, hospital in October 1983. Her parents' first doctor recommended immediate surgery but they decided not to have it after talking to Dr. George Newman, a neurologist at Stony Brook hospital. Among other things, Dr. Newman told them that Baby Jane had "virtually a 100 percent chance of being retarded."

It is almost certain that Dr. Newman was wrong. He thought Jane's head was abnormally small, but another, more exerienced surgeon testified that it was in the normal size range. Nevertheless, Baby Jane's parents stuck to their decision. As a result, Baby Jane will probably be retarded after all, her life will almost certainly be shorter, and she will definitely be crippled.[10]

Eric Scuterud's story is happier, no thanks to some of his doctors. Eric was born in Yale-New Haven Medical Center with spina bifida. Some of Eric's doctors told his parents that the boy should not have the corrective surgery because he would be physically and possibly mentally impaired. They even suggested that his nourishment be withdrawn.

At one point, doctors offered to let Eric go home to die. They would give his mother, a trained nurse, enough morphine to sedate him so he would not cry for food.

Eric's parents resisted this advice and ordered an operation for their son. He did well. He may never walk without braces, but his intelligence is normal.[11]

Some of these cases illustrate another feature of modern infanticide: doctors are active participants. In medieval Europe, parents turned unwanted infants over to disreputable "wet nurses" from the lower classes, with the understanding that these women would "take care" of the problem. Today, it is often physicians who do the gruesome work. Some of them are quite willing to initiate the deed.

One day Dr. Milton Heifetz, chief of neurosugery at a Los Angeles hospital, was called in to examine an infant girl born with spina bifida. The baby was her parents' first; they were stricken with grief to learn that she would never walk normally and might be mentally impaired as well. Dr. Heifetz realized he could fix the opening in their daughter's spine and save her life, but he decided to be "completely open and truthful" with them. He describes the encounter:

> I said that during the first few months of life the child would be like every other infant who does not walk. As she got older, she would be able to move only by dragging herself on the floor by her arms. She would spend most of her days on the floor or in a chair. Her later life would be in a wheelchair or, at most, on crutches dragging her legs. She probably would be mentally retarded in spite of surgery to drain the fluid damaging her brain.
>
> I explained all the alternatives to the family.

The shocked parents were confused by all this. Dr. Heifetz thought they agreed with him—that the girl should not leave the hospital alive—but they could not bring themselves to order their daughter's death. Dr. Heifetz offered to help. "I therefore suggested that they allow me to make the decision for them. To do what I believed was best. They agreed." He did not operate, and the girl died "within three weeks."[12]

Another group of infants specially targeted for infanticide are those who survive abortions. The Center for Disease Control estimates that 500 of the 1.5 million abortions in the U.S. each year result in the birth of live, viable babies. These abortions are "failures" in the women's minds. The abortionist-physicians tend to view them that way too. Some take steps to finish the job.

An unnamed black male baby died in Boston City Hospital in the fall of 1974 after he survived an abortion. He was "delivered" by Dr. Kenneth Edelin, the hospital's chief resident in obstetrics and gynecology, in an abortion procedure called a hysterotomy. The baby's mother was anesthetized, and Dr. Edelin made an incision in the womb and pulled the baby out. He then put the boy in a stainless steel basin which a scrub nurse emptied into a container in a back room. But the 1 lb. 8½ oz. boy was very much alive. The medical examiner later determined that he died of lack of oxygen. Dr. Edelin had done nothing to help him breathe.

Dr. Edelin was convicted of manslaughter, but his conviction was reversed by the Supreme Judicial Court of Massachusetts. The appeals court decided that a baby's death is presumed in an abortion and that a physician has no obligation to care for a child that he believes is dead. Neither, apparently, does he have an obligation to see if the baby is alive.[13]

How frequently does infanticide occur? Is it an isolated tragedy, or a bloody assault on whole groups of handicapped infants?

The answer to this question deeply influences what we can

do to stop it. It is virtually impossible to prevent isolated murderous acts against newborns. However, a pattern of infanticide—a readiness among professionals to act against certain types of babies—can be the focus of public policy initiatives.

It is impossible to come up with a precise figure. A total of 45,945 babies died in 1978. The Public Health Service, of course, does not list "infanticide" as one of the causes of infant death in its annual infant mortality statistics. (It did record 161 homicides, however.)[14]

Infanticide is a secret crime. For obvious reasons, hospitals do not record it as a cause of death. Parents of dead children do not talk much about decisions they have made. Nurses are silent about what they see and are sometimes ordered to do. Their careers are at stake.

Doctors, however, are not entirely close-mouthed about what happens to handicapped infants. Physicians who have spoken out about the practice have done so for one of three reasons: 1) to deplore the discriminatory withholding of treatment; 2) to break the silence about what goes on and appeal for a more "liberal" policy; and 3) to resist the federal government's attempts to provide civil rights protection for handicapped newborns.

Physicians in the last group tend to deny that infanticide happens frequently. Doctors who deplore it or call for its acceptance usually say it happens all the time.

The American Academy of Pediatrics bitterly opposed the federal government's Baby Doe regulations, first proposed in 1983 and issued in final form in 1984. Dr. George Little, an official of the Academy, told a Senate subcommittee in 1983 that "there is no evidence to justify the assumption that hospitals are routinely treating babies inappropriately."[15]

By contrast, Dr. Raymond Duff of Yale-New Haven, who also opposed the rules, says that at any given time two or three infants in his special care nursery are candidates for death. Dr. Duff also maintains that his readiness to withhold treatment is widely shared by physicians in neonatal intensive care units. (We will hear more from Dr. Duff and other pro-infanticide physicians in later chapters.)

Surgeon General C. Everett Koop, thinks federal regulations might save as many as 1,200 babies each year. Dr. Koop is also a leading pediatric surgeon who, upon receiving the American Academy of Pediatrics' highest honor in 1976, told the assembled pediatricians in his acceptance address: "You all know that infanticide is being practiced right now in this country." (We will hear more from Dr. Koop later.)

Other knowledgeable observers reach conclusions closer to Koop's and Duff's than to Little's.

B.D. Cohen, medical writer for *Newsday*, says: "The decision to withhold or withdraw treatment from extremely sick, premature, and/or deformed newborns is probably being made at least once every day by anguished parents and doctors in one of the nation's more than 500 intensive care nurseries."[16]

A doctor at the hospital where Infant Doe should have had his surgery was not surprised that the baby never came. "It happens all too frequently," said Dr. Joseph Christian, chairman of medical genetics at Riley Memorial Hospital in Indianapolis. "I've been involved in a number of cases when the parents have made that decision."[17]

"It's extremely common, it happens every day," said Dr. Alan Fleischman, director of the division of neonatology at Albert Einstein College of Medicine in New York City.[18]

Knowledgeable as people like these are, they are still giving impressions. Is there any data available to back up their assertions?

There seems to be. For a secret crime, a surprisingly large number of infanticide cases, or attempts at infanticide, have become known one way or another. Many of these cases are cited in this book.

Further evidence comes from the government's "Baby Doe"

telephone notification system. The Department of Health and Human Services Office for Civil Rights (OCR) set up the toll-free service in March 1983 to receive reports of suspected discriminatory nontreatment of handicapped babies. Over the next six months, OCR received forty-nine complaints from all over the country, from large cities and rural towns, from large medical centers and small hospitals.[19] Here is a sampling of the complaints:

—San Francisco: A complaint that a baby with a cleft palate and a heart defect had been allowed to die in a hospital. Caller said a malpractice lawsuit was pending.

—Boynton Beach, Florida: complaint that two handicapped infants were allowed to die immediately after birth.

—Duarte, California: a parent complains that a hospital would not admit a boy for a bone marrow transplant because he had Down's syndrome.

—San Antonio: complaint that many children at two hospitals had been discriminatorily denied care. The local district attorney asked HHS to postpone its investigation because a grand jury was looking into it.

—Newark, New Jersey: complaint that a baby born as a result of a third trimester abortion was not receiving care. After an immediate on-site investigation, the baby was resuscitated and appropriate care was provided.

—Houston: complaint that five infants were being denied proper care in a neonatal intensive care unit.

—Jackson, Michigan: a mother complains that her son, who had Down's syndrome, died as a result of improper treatment.

In three other cases, complaints led to investigations that may well have saved the lives of babies born with spina bifida.

On May 14, 1982, OCR received a complaint that a hospital in Robinson, Illinois, had failed to perform surgery on a spina bifida infant. OCR, the Justice Department, and a state agency investigated. When the parents continued to refuse treatment, the state took custody of the child, had successful surgery performed, and arranged for his adoption.

On May 19, 1983, OCR received a complaint that parents of a spina bifida infant in Daytona Beach, Florida, had refused corrective surgery. The information turned out to be true. The surgery was performed on May 22 under a court order obtained by the state of Florida.

Almost a month later, on June 21, a nurse in Colorado Springs complained that another spina bifida infant was being denied surgery. An OCR medical consultant went to the hospital and discovered that the physicians were delaying the operation. The surgery was performed that evening after the consultant discussed the case with doctors and told them the Justice Department would be notified.

The mere fact that a complaint was made does not mean that the parents, physicians, and hospitals involved were guilty of infanticide. But the telephone system did uncover considerable smoke and some fire. It provides further evidence that the danger facing impaired newborns is real.

A final way to indicate the extent of the problem is to determine how many babies are at risk. Not all handicapped babies are mistreated, but there are many thousands of infants born with the kind of handicaps that cause parents and physicians to ask "*Should* we treat?"

Many thousands of American infants come into the world far from "perfect." In 1979, 3,473,000 children were born in the U.S. Between 1 and 2 percent of these infants were born with some kind of hereditary malformation—ranging from cleft palate to Down's syndrome. Some 250,000 of these babies need special medical treatment ranging in duration from a few days to months. There are 7,500 intensive care beds in U.S. hospital nurseries. The cost of neonatal intensive care is somewhere between $1.5 billion and $3 billion annually.[20]

It is not easy to determine how many of these newborns might so distress their parents and physicians that they would be starved, unplugged from life-support systems, refused an operation, or sedated until they quietly die. Different authorities classify birth defects differently. Babies with moderate impairments are listed with infants with more severe disabilities. Not all disabilities are recorded.

Let us look at the classes of more severe impairments—chromosomal disorders (including Down's syndrome), severe disorders of the central nervous system (including spina bifida), and severe disorders of the muscles and skeleton.

Working from data recorded on birth certificates, the Center for Disease Control estimates that in every 10,000 births, 8.1 infants are born with Down's syndrome, 17.8 have severe central nervous system disabilities, and 18 have serious musculoskeletal impairments.[21] At 1979 birth rates, the Center's figures would yield an annual total of 15,246 babies in the categories that make many parents and doctors wonder about "quality of life."

The real figure is almost certainly far higher. Birth certificate data gives a limited picture of the true incidence of birth defects. A long-term study of nearly 17,000 babies born in the San Francisco Bay area found an incidence of birth defects nearly three times the rate reported by the Center for Disease Control.[22] Figured according to the San Francisco data, the rate of birth defects, based on 1979 birth rates,would be 10,071 babies with chromosomal defects, 20,838 with severe central nervous system disorders, and 13,892 with serious musculoskeletal defects. Total: 44,801 handicapped babies.

The Center for Disease Control figures would have 42 children a day born with serious impairments. The San Francisco data would mean 122 children a day. The average: 82 children a day born at risk of infanticide.

Are these babies truly at risk? Are people really prepared to kill them? To answer that question, we must look at what doctors have been saying about infanticide since the early 1970s.

THREE

To Cure or to Kill?

"The profession of medicine must keep some socially useful or necessary legal and religious doctrines a little distance away."
—Dr. Raymond S. Duff

I N 1972, A PROMINENT PHYSICIAN used the popular press to bring infanticide into public view. He was Dr. Anthony Shaw, a pediatric surgeon at the University of Virginia Medical Center. His forum was an influential organ—the Sunday *New York Times Magazine*.[1] The title of his article was in the form of a question Dr. Shaw said he often heard from parents of handicapped newborns who needed life-sustaining treatment—"Doctor, Do We Have a Choice?"

His answer was yes.

Dr. Shaw was not writing about gravely ill babies or those struggling for life against multiple severe disabilities. His article was about mentally impaired infants, specifically those with Down's syndrome. More precisely, he was concerned about the successful, ambitious *parents* of mentally impaired infants. These parents are often distraught when presented with a child "whose maximum achievement might be the ability to write his own name."

Such parents often withhold consent for life-saving surgery, Dr. Shaw reported. He would do the same: "If it were my own child I would refuse to allow any measures other than simple procedures to relieve terminal suffering."

These infants usually starve to death. The manner of death bothers Dr. Shaw: "As a surgeon whose natural inclination is to use the scalpel to fight off death, standing by and watching a salvageable baby die is the most emotionally exhausting experience I know."

The medical literature of the following decade held many shocks for people who thought that physicians always went to bat for babies in tough spots.

A year after Dr. Shaw's article, Dr. Raymond Duff and Dr. A.G.M. Campbell reported that 14 percent of the infant deaths in their intensive care nursery at Yale-New Haven Hospital were caused by deliberate withholding or withdrawal of treatment.

A majority of pediatricians and pediatric surgeons answering a national survey said they would not treat a baby like Infant Doe if the parents wanted him to die.

Half the pediatricians answering surveys in Massachusetts and in the San Francisco Bay area would not operate on a Down's syndrome baby with an intestinal obstruction. A third of the pediatricians thought they should be allowed to kill such infants directly.

It was reported that most spina bifida babies in Great Britain and many in the U.S. do not receive corrective and life-saving surgery because physicians and parents think their quality of life would be too low.

In 1974, seventeen of twenty medical professionals and bioethecists meeting in Sonoma Valley, California, said they would support direct killing of infants in some circumstances. Only one member of this elite group flatly opposed direct killing.

These events seemed to reflect a deep change in the thinking of the nation's pediatricians. All the material just cited was duly published in medical journals read by other physicians. Some protested what they read, but there was no public outcry. Of course, many physicians continued to treat handicapped babies humanely. But a new ethic seemed to be taking hold of the profession's opinion-molders.

Evidence that the new ethic had spread came in the wake of the Infant Doe case. When the government warned that hospitals were not to tolerate discrimination against disabled newborns, physicians and medical administrators protested. The American Academy of Pediatrics got a federal judge to strike down the first "Baby Doe regulations." When the government invited comments on revised rules, 72 percent of the pediatricians who commented opposed them.

Dr. Shaw illustrated various facets of the new ethic in a 1973 article published in *The New England Journal of Medicine*.[2] He presented a number of cases to illustrate ethical problems in the practice of pediatric surgery. Five of the cases involved decisions about whether to keep mentally impaired infants alive.

Baby A was a Down's syndrome infant with a problem much like Infant Doe's. The parents reluctantly consented to surgery and immediately sent the baby to a state institution. Dr. Shaw commented: "If their intention is to place the baby after operation in a state-funded institution, should the initial decision regarding medical and surgical treatment for their infant be theirs alone?"

Baby B's problems were similar to Baby A's. His parents refused surgery after the hospital ran a chromosome test confirming the presence of Down's syndrome. The baby starved to death in three days.

Baby C's fate was the same as Baby B's. In this case, however, the physician-father asked Dr. Shaw what *he* would do if the baby were his. Dr. Shaw admitted that he wouldn't order the operation either.

Baby D's grandfather called Dr. Shaw to tell him about his grandson. The two-week-old Down's syndrome baby was slowly dying of uremic poisoning in a New York hospital. The parents wanted him to die and refused corrective surgery; the hospital staff resisted their decision and insisted that the parents take the child out of the hospital. Dr. Shaw asked: "Can we prepare hospital, medical and paramedical personnel to accept the death of infants under these circumstances without the destruction of morale?"

Baby E, another Down's syndrome infant, survived because a court ordered surgery to repair an intestinal obstruction. Her mother, partner in "an already shaky marriage," had refused surgery and wanted the baby to die. Eighteen months later the mother felt she had been done a great injustice. Dr. Shaw wonders whether child abuse laws were properly applied in this case.

Here was the new attitude: the suggestion that society has an interest in seeing certain babies die (Baby A), the prejudice against the mentally impaired (Baby B), the physician's personal sympathy with the parents (Baby C), the concern to get other medical personnel on board (Baby D), and the suggestion that the law is too harsh (Baby E). Nowhere in this article did Dr. Shaw deal with the *baby's* rights and interests.

How many doctors share this attitude? Does Dr. Shaw represent fringe views or a wider ethic in the profession?

He does not seem to be alone. Revealing data on this question comes from a survey of the attitudes of pediatric surgeons and pediatricians, published in 1977 in the journal *Pediatrics*.[3] It was a scientifically sound study: the survey was well-designed and the response rate was high. The results are considered reliable. In all, 267 pediatric surgeons and 190 pediatricians answered questions about how they would deal with various medical and ethical issues that arose in the treatment of handicapped and disabled newborns.

This is a summary of what the pediatricians said.

1. *Should the life of every newborn be saved if medicine could do so?* Only 17 percent of the surgeons and 19 percent of the pediatricians thought so.

2. *Whose lives are not worth saving?* Large majorities would

not fight for a Down's syndrome or spina bifida child. 76.8 percent of the surgeons would not perform life-saving surgery on a Down's syndrome infant if the parents refused consent. 60.3 percent would withhold such surgery on a child with spina bifida if the parents wished.

3. *At what point would surgeons oppose parents' wishes in such matters?* Fifty-four percent would insist on surgery only if the child was normal—that is, free of *any* disabling condition. Even then, their opposition would be muted: only 3 percent would go so far as to get a court order for surgery. Astoundingly, 8 percent said they would *never* oppose the parents; they would not act to save *even a normal child* if its parents wished to let it die.

4. *How would doctors conduct themselves in the crucial discussions with the parents of a handicapped baby?* Only 17 percent of the surgeons would try to persuade the parents to allow surgery. Almost a quarter (23.6 percent) would try to get the parents to refuse surgery. Half the surgeons would take an ostensibly neutral role. They would tell the parents everything they knew about the infant's condition and then leave the decision up to them.

5. *What would the surgeon do if his or her own handicapped child needed an operation?* Two-thirds of the surgeons would refuse to have surgery done on their own Down's syndrome child to repair an intestinal obstruction. (Among these, of course, are some of the surgeons who said they would be "neutral" in their conversations with parents of such infants. One wonders how neutral such doctors can truly be.)

6. *What would doctors do with handicapped infants after the decision has been made to let them die?* This problem troubled some surgeons. Sixty-three percent would stop all supportive treatment, including intravenous feeding, and starve the child to death. Yet 30 percent would continue oral feedings—"to ease the burden of stress and conscience on the nurses," one surgeon wrote on his questionnaire.

Two other surveys in the medical literature fill out and

confirm this picture of physicians' attitudes. A survey of 230 pediatricians in Massachusetts found that 51 percent thought that an infant with problems like Infant Doe's should not be operated on.[4] Only one-third would recommend surgery for a spina bifida infant who is likely to be severely disabled. Thirty-two percent wished the law permitted them to kill infants in certain circumstances.

A study of pediatricians and obstetricians in the San Francisco Bay area found that 22 percent favored "active or passive euthanasia" in the case of a Down's syndrome baby born *with no complications*. If the baby also had an intestinal obstruction, 50 percent would withhold surgey and let the baby die. The study director commented that "some physicians chose to view a relatively simple operation as an insurmountable barrier."[5]

If these attitudes predict actual behavior, it would be naive to think that Infant Doe's death was unusual. With parents like his, convinced that a Down's syndrome child cannot have an acceptable quality of life, he would have died in many hospitals in the United States. Babies like him undoubtedly have. In fact, the pediatricians at Bloomington Hospital were more humane than the majority who answered the *Pediatrics* survey. They *opposed* the "non-treatment" of Infant Doe.

In 1981, an eminent pediatrician, arguing for letting handicapped babies die, appealed for freedom for medical people to go their own way. "The profession of medicine," he wrote, "often must keep some socially useful or necessary legal and religious doctrines a little distance away."[6]

To better understand the change that has come over the medical profession, let us take a closer look at the man who wrote those words—Dr. Raymond Duff of Yale-New Haven Hospital.

Dr. Duff co-authored the famous article which first described infanticide as a standard medical practice. Its title was

"Moral and Ethical Dilemmas in the Special-Care Nursery" and it was published in 1973 in the prestigous *New England Journal of Medicine.*[7]

The impeccable credentials of the authors guaranteed that the article would have an immediate impact. Both Dr. Duff and his co-author, Dr. A.G.M. Campbell, had shared the duties of physician in charge of patient care and teaching in the special-care nursery at Yale-New Haven Hospital, an outstanding neonatal facility attached to a major medical school. Dr. Duff was also professor of pediatrics at Yale Medical School. He was (and is) a physician with that unique combination of clinical skill, teaching experience, and research support that makes him a leader in his medical speciality.

Drs. Duff and Campbell described a pattern of infanticide in their unit. They revealed that 14 percent of the deaths in the special care nursery over a thirty-six-month period were caused by deliberate decisions to withhold or withdraw treatment. Two-hundred and ninety-nine babies died in all. Most of them were born dying or died despite treatment. Forty-three babies were allowed to die because doctors withheld or withdrew treatment.

They gave examples. A boy with Down's syndrome and a malformed intestinal tract was denied surgery because "his parents thought that surgery was wrong for their baby and themselves."

A girl with spina bifida was denied surgery "when the parents understood the limits of medical care and rehabilitation."

It is not unreasonable to suspect that both these infants may have been denied food and water as well as surgery, because they both died within days.

A third baby, a five-month-old, died three hours after oxygen supplementation was withdrawn. The reason: the hospital bill was already over $15,000 and "the strains of the illness were believed to be threatening the marriage bonds and to be causing sibling behavioral disturbances."

Why did these three babies and forty others die? Here is a sampling of some of the terms Dr. Duff employed to describe the reasons:

—"Parents and physicians in a group decision concluded that prognosis for meaningful life was extremely poor or hopeless."

—"Some thought their child had a right to die since he could not live well or effectively."

—"Such very defective individuals were considered to have little or no hope of achieving meaningful 'humanhood.'"

—"They have little or no capacity to love or be loved."

—"To escape 'wrongful life,' a fate rated as worse than death, seemed right."

—"Families . . . feared that they . . . would become socially enslaved, economically deprived, and permanently stigmatized."

Bear in mind that Dr. Duff is not talking about dying babies, or even for the most part about "hard cases"—infants whose ultimate capacity to perceive the outside world and interact with it will be genuinely minimal. He is saying these terrible things about babies who have Down's syndrome or spina bifida, like some children in your neighborhood, in your local school, or even somewhere in your own family.

Babies born with spina bifida often become targets for infanticide. During the 1970s, a controversy erupted on both sides of the Atlantic about how to treat these children. Some specialists have proposed that most of these infants be left to die. They have left us with a well-documented picture of infanticide.

Spina bifida is both hard to treat and hard to live with. It is one of the most common birth defects. About two infants in every thousand are born with it, making spina bifida much more common than such better-known neurological disorders as polio, muscular dystrophy, and multiple sclerosis.

This condition, known technically as meningocele or myelomeningocele, is a spinal lesion which leaves about 90 percent of its victims with some degree of physical disability. To prevent greater disability, it is usually important to surgically close the hole in the spine immediately after birth. Closure, however, can lead to hydrocephalus (water on the brain) which in turn can cause brain damage if not relieved by a shunt. Aggressive treatment can be expensive, time-consuming, and stressful. Even with successful therapy, most spina bifida children will become disabled adults. Thus they are likely candidates for infanticide.

However, those who would rather be rid of such babies cannot easily rely on the option of "nontreatment." If the wound is left open, meningitis often develops, and, unless treated with antibiotics, the baby will die. However, some spina bifida victims will survive neglect and live on with much more severe disabilities than if they had been treated aggressively.

"A policy of so-called 'benign neglect' is both offensive and ineffective," says Dr. David McLone, the foremost American specialist in the treatment of spina bifida.[8]

The man who tried to solve the spina bifida "problem" was an Englishman, Dr. John Lorber of Children's Hospital in Sheffield. Throughout the 1960s, British doctors had been aggressively treating these children with new therapies. But they were creating a large number of disabled people.

Dr. Lorber thought that most disabled spina bifida victims should be weeded out at birth. Only infants with the best chance of achieving good mobility and escaping mental impairment should be treated, he said. The others should not be treated.[9] His "selective nontreatment" approach subsequently found wide acceptance on both sides of the Atlantic. In Britain today, only 25 percent of spina bifida infants have surgery and receive aggressive medical care.[10]

What happens to those infants not treated? The answer is not pleasant.

Dr. R.B. Zachary, a colleague of Dr. Lorber's, found it curious that the mortality rate for infants not selected for surgery was usually 100 percent. How can this be when the spinal lesion itself is rarely a fatal condition? Dr. Zachary discovered the answer:

> These babies are receiving 60 mg/kg body weight of chloral hydrate, not once, but four times a day. This is eight times the sedative dose of chloral hydrate recommended in the most recent volume of *Nelson's Paediatrics* and four times the hypnotic dose, and it is being administered four times every day. No wonder these babies are sleepy and demand no feed, and with this regimen most of them will die within a few weeks, many within the first week.[11]

Dr. Zachary recounts a conference with pediatricians in a medical center where only one out of twenty-four spina bifida infants were operated on and where all the others died:

> When asked, "Did they fall or were they pushed"—into death—the reply was, "They were pushed of course." At another meeting I attended a paediatrician was asked by a medical student what was his method of management, and the reply was, "We don't feed them."[12]

Some British physicians joke about putting such babies on "a low calorie diet."

In an American medical journal, Dr. Lorber explained exactly how infants not selected for surgery were to be cared for:

> If the object of selective nontreatment is the early, painless death of the infant, then one must do nothing to prolong

life. This means no antibiotic therapy for infections, no "intensive care," no oxygen or tube feeding and infants should be fed on demand, no more.[13]

Dr. Lorber's "selective nontreatment" of spina bifida infants is not as common in the United States as it is in Great Britain, but it has its advocates here too.

Some American advocates of spina bifida "nontreatment" are quite influential.

In their paper describing infant deaths at Yale-New Haven Hospital, Dr. Duff and Dr. Campbell admit that spina bifida was a special concern. Many physicians and families grew to dislike the standard policy of treating these infants aggressively; too many lived on with severe physical and mental impairments. Neglect was unsatisfactory too; death came slowly and cruelly. "What were the most appropriate medical responses?" Duff and Campbell ask ominously.

They do not answer their question directly, but seven of the forty-three infants who were allowed to die in their unit were spina bifida babies. One of them died at five days of age, quite early for an infant with a condition that is rarely fatal in itself.

Dr. Milton Heifetz also rejects aggressive treatment of spina bifida. He thinks physicians should identify spina bifida babies who will certainly die without treatment, and agree not to treat them.[14]

Dr. William Taeusch, chief of neonatology at Harvard University's Bringham and Women's Hospital, is another prominent physician who favors "the British criteria" in treatment of spina bifida.[15]

In October 1983, a group of Oklahoma physicians published a paper in *Pediatrics* describing a selection process whereby they decided not to operate on twenty-four spina bifida babies. The unlucky infants were transferred to a suburban home converted into an "intermediate care" facility where they were fed but not treated with antibiotics to attack the inevitable infections. Not suprisingly, all twenty-four babies died.[16]

"Selective nontreatment" sounds objective and clinical, but it has little to do with medical judgments. Even if doctors could precisely identify those spina bifida babies who will be severely disabled adults (something most specialists insist cannot be done) they would still be making value judgments about the worth of human lives.

Even though their deaths are welcomed, the way some handicapped children die bothers some physicians greatly. The "nontreatment option" usually means a slow death by infection or starvation—a manner of death most people consider barbaric. Thus it is not surprising that some doctors long for the authority to kill infants directly—to administer the lethal injection.

One physician who looks at the question very coolly is Dr. J. Alex Haller, chief of neonatology at Johns Hopkins Medical Center. "If we can decide there are indications for not allowing a child to survive," he says, "then the humane and ethical way of handling that would be to come up with some sort of way of immediately allowing them to die. You can make it a little bit more striking by saying—some way to kill them."[17]

Dr. Haller participated in one of the most gruesome infanticide cases to become publicly known—the fifteen-day starvation death of a Down's syndrome boy at Johns Hopkins Medical Center in 1970.

Dr. Haller admits that the film later made about the case depicts a "manslaughter." But he explains that "by our traditions in the medical profession and our ethical traditions generally, we don't have any way we can kill a child in the sense of injecting something."[18]

These traditions are coming under pressure. The 1977 survey of physicians' attitudes found several doctors who longed for the legal authority to administer a lethal injection. "[Lethal injection] is what I would prefer to do but it is illegal under present laws," wrote one pediatrician. A surgeon commented that starvation "is barbaric but best without legal authority." He too thought a lethal injection was "most humane."[19]

Another survey found that 32 percent of pediatricians in Massachusetts thought the law should be changed to allow direct killing of infants under certain circumstances.[20]

Dr. John Freeman, a Johns Hopkins neonatologist, thinks that most spina bifida infants should be treated because it is illegal to kill them directly. "Active euthanasia might be the most humane course for the *most severely* affected infants," he writes. "Until active euthanasia, with whatever appropriate safeguards, becomes acceptable to society, I feel that vigorous treatment should be pursued for *virtually* every case."[21]

If this is the rationale for treatment, can direct killing be far behind?

Indeed, physicians have been accused of killing infants directly.

In 1983, a Canadian court acquitted a doctor of a murder charge for administering large doses of morphine to a disabled infant. The court found that the doctor did indeed order the morphine; the problem was that it could not be legally established that the sedative caused the child's death.

A Down's syndrome infant was born on June 28, 1980 in an English hospital. An autopsy after his death, sixty-nine hours after he was born, found that the baby had more than enough sedative in his blood to kill a full-sized adult. Dr. Leonard Arthur, the attending physician, had administered the drugs and written on the baby's chart "Parents do not wish it to survive. Nursing care only." He, too, was acquitted of murder.[22]

Is there really a distinction between direct and indirect killing? Is it worse to kill by injecting morphine than to starve a Down's syndrome baby to death? Is it more "direct" to put a handicapped baby into a terminal coma with sedatives than to let it succumb to an infection that could be successfully treated with antibiotics? These are some of the questions doctors are beginning to ask as the medical profession enters a brave new world.

The lives of the eighty-two or so babies born each day with disabilities do indeed seem to be at risk in many places in the United States. The reason is not their medical condition but the attitudes of their doctors. Infants with significant handicaps cannot know whether the physician is approaching to cure or to kill.

FOUR

Doctors and Decisions

"Telling me I should kill my daughter! I would have killed him before I killed my daughter, if my friend wasn't there. 'Cause I had my hand half-cocked and this is when my friend pulled me out of the room."

—Ted Mekdeci, describing an
encounter with Dr. Raymond S. Duff

P HYSICIANS HAVE GREAT INFLUENCE over life-and-death decisions in the newborn nursery. In fact, it is largely a pious sentiment to argue, as many do, that parents should make the tough calls about the lives of their disabled offspring. Doctors make many of these decisions on their own. When they talk to parents, they can usually find a way to guide the decision along the path they think best.

Dr. Milton Heifetz, the Los Angeles neurosurgeon, tells a story.

A couple brought their three-month-old daughter to him for examination. She was hydrocephalic, brain damaged, and blind. She needed surgery to reduce fluid build-up in the brain as well as antibiotics for recurrent ear infections.

In the course of his examination and discussion with the parents, Dr. Heifetz noticed something: the mother was very attentive to the child and "somewhat abrupt with her husband." He discovered that the husband did not want the surgery performed, although he was willing to go along with whatever his wife wanted.

Dr. Heifetz decided to be helpful. "I was certain the mother agreed with the logic of her husband but was emotionally unable to face it," he writes. "I could not accept her approach as honest. I suggested surgery be withheld, as well as all other medical support, including antibiotics for the recurrent ear infection." This child died "within months."

Dr. Heifetz believes that parents should make decisions about treating their handicapped babies, but adds a qualifier. "If there is difficulty reaching a decision, I do not hesitate to ask for the right to make the decision for them," he admits.

What about his colleagues? Says Dr. Heifetz: "There are many physicians, including myself, who have simply told parents that the case of a newborn is hopeless and that nothing could be done, when procedures were possible but life would be meaningless."[1]

The official view is that parents are supposed to make these decisions. As a presidential commission said, "parents are best situated to collaborate with practitioners in making decisions about an infant's care...parents are usually present, concerned, willing to become informed."[2] As we shall see, parental authority in these matters is hardly absolute, nor should it be. But parents should not be manipulated, kept in the dark, or even lied to by physicians bent on disposing of disabled infants.

Doctors who do these things risk a malpractice suit. Thus, when consultation does take place in the intensive care nursery, it is often to make sure that the parents will not sue if they later come to regret their baby's death. One study of the doctor-parent relationship concluded that "consultation with the family is used in part as a method of insuring that they will accept the decision and not take legal action against the physician later. It is not considered appropriate for the family to make the final decision."[3]

Survey data confirms these impressions.

Fully a third of the pediatricians and pediatric surgeons answering the national survey thought doctors should decide whether handicapped newborns should be treated. (A sizeable minority thought a hospital committee should shoulder this responsibility.) Nearly a quarter of the surgeons took a position somewhat like Dr. Heifetz.' They would "move [the parents] in the direction of not signing [consent for surgery], making the decision to let the baby die [their] own."

Many physicians wrote marginal comments on the survey forms which make a few common sense points: doctors are powerful authority figures, and parents are often poorly equipped to make difficult decisions in the wake of the birth of a handicapped baby.

A surgeon commented: "I believe parents' decisions are almost *always* influenced by the physician's presentation, objective as we may attempt to be."

Said another: "I find myself helping parents form the decision which seems right for their situation, rather than 'acquiesce' to their decision."

Another wrote that "acquiescence or nonacquiescence is putting it too simply. The manner in which the problem is presented to the parents is going to have a distinct bearing on their decision."

Dr. Raymond S. Duff of Yale-New Haven is an expert at presenting problems to parents. Dr. Duff portrays himself as an advocate for parents' freedom to be rid of handicapped babies. Yet he hedges his declaration about parental prerogatives. He never says that parents have the sole authority to make treatment decisions. Instead, parents must *share* decision-making with physicians. The parents are part of a team which includes physicians, house officers, nurses, and social workers. When medical people disagree about care, the family "may then *help* to resolve the conflict" (emphasis added).[4]

How does this "team" work in practice?

The atmosphere in the special care nursery is "emotionally

charged," Duff and Campbell write. Two to three babies die every week. All the infants are seriously ill, many for long periods of time. Many will never lead normal lives.

Some parents of these unfortunate newborns are knowledgeable, professional people—"physicians, nurses, lawyers,"—who seek relief from "seemingly pointless, crushing burdens" of the continued care of such children. The medical staff can understand and accomodate these desires. Treatment is discontinued.

However, other parents are not so knowledgeable. They do not suspect that their children have a "right to die." They do not come to the doctors asking that treatment be discontinued.

For Duff and Campbell, these "less knowledgeable" parents are *the* problem in the special care nursery. The problem is not taking life. The assumption is that these babies should not live. (Duff and Campbell describe no case where treatment of a handicapped newborn is successfully sustained.) Rather, the challenge is to get morally unsophisticated parents to *agree* that these babies should not live.

This, write Duff and Campbell in *The New England Journal of Medicine*, is a problem for *physicians*. Most would let their own handicapped children die and they usually go along with knowledgeable parents who desire death for their struggling babies. Yet they are reluctant to bring up the "nontreatment" option to parents who might not think of it themselves.

Duff and Campbell think this reluctance is wrong. "The physician's failure to face the issues may constitute a victimizing abandonment of patients and their families in times of greatest need," they write. They suggest that responsible physicians would help these parents see the advantages to themselves of letting their infants die or even causing them to die.

This, apparently, is precisely what Duff and Campbell did at Yale-New Haven. "Our almost constant availability to staff, private pediatricians and parents," they write in the abstract language of journal prose, "has resulted in the raising of more and more ethical questions about various aspects of intensive care for critically ill and congenitally deformed infants."

If the idea of letting babies die does not occur to parents, Duff and Campbell bring it up. When the death decision has to be made, the doctor is in charge: "the physician takes appropriate initiative in final decision making."

In Duff's later writing, it becomes clear that his main crusade is not freedom for parents but freedom for physicians to practice a new kind of medicine based on cost-benefit calculations and bias against the handicapped. He questions the motives of physicians who would give medical care to the seriously handicapped who need treatment urgently.

"It is very difficult to know whether an intervening person is a knight riding to rescue the helpless, an anxious person who understandably seeks only self-protection, or one who seeks some idiosyncratic advantage," he told a congressional committee.[5] These physicians, he disingenuously remarks, are paternalistic.

Dr. Duff deplores "rigid" policies in some nurseries that insist on court review of nontreatment decisions and proscribe actions that hasten a child's death. Those responsible for such policies are afraid of the homicide laws, seduced by "the appealing ethics of the crusade against disease and death," and concerned to protect "institutional license and finances and jobs." They are "moral entrepreneurs."[6]

This is a breathtaking rhetorical offensive. Bear in mind that these fearful, paternalistic, advantage-seeking, job-protecting moral entrepreneurs are physicians who uphold the law, the highest traditions of the medical profession, and the right of helpless infants to live. For Dr. Duff, they are the enemy. "Does anyone want to be forced to live in circumstances which they or their loved ones believe are intolerable?" he asks.[7]

The issue, in Dr. Duff's eyes, is nothing less than righteous defiance of oppressive laws. "Neither coercive living nor coercive dying has any place in a free society," he writes. "Some coercive living under oppressive conditions must be endured unless individuals prompted by compassion and conscience engage in risky acts of disobedience."[8]

Those who need to defend the oppressed are doctors. Dr. Duff calls on the medical profession to take hold of its responsibility to "establish a standard of conduct for itself and to assert the freedom to do what it considers best."[9]

Dr. Duff follows his own advice. He is not bashful about telling others what he thinks they should do.

In 1983, television reporters working on a documentary about infanticide interviewed two couples who ran across Dr. Duff in the Yale-New Haven special care nursery.

Leo and Irene Arria's son Jimmy was born prematurely and spent eighteen days in the intensive care unit at Yale-New Haven. Without being asked, Leo said, Dr. Duff told them that Jimmy would be "a vegetable and that we should let him go." Jimmy is perfectly normal today.

Ted Mekdeci's daughter Kimberly was born with spina bifida. Ted said that Dr. Duff offered unsolicited advice to let the girl die. "He said that Kim would probably grow up to be a vegetable, her life would be meaningless," Mekdeci angrily told the reporters. Kim also is doing just fine today. She is not a vegetable.

Ted Mekdeci rebuffed Dr. Duff with a certain flair. As he described it on television: "Telling me I should kill my daughter! I would have killed *him* before I killed my daughter, if my friend wasn't there. 'Cause I had my hand half-cocked and this is when my friend pulled me out of the room."[10]

In 1981, a reporter for *The Hartford Courant* uncovered evidence that doctors at Yale-New Haven sometimes send parents of handicapped infants home with enough sedatives to give them a lethal overdose. The parents were given morphine if they were able to administer injections. If not, they received crystalline phenobarbital to dissolve in the baby's formula. The doctor who explained the procedure to the reporter said that all such deaths he knew about occurred at home, but that he "wouldn't discount its happening in the hospital."[11]

Duff, Shaw, Heifetz, and other advocates of infanticide-on-demand portray parents of handicapped newborns as despairing people who are forever thankful when a sensitive (and courageous) physician articulates their secret desires and arranges their babies' deaths.

The truth is far different.

For one thing, a decision for death is not always firm. Infant Doe's parents may have been resolute, but not all parents are. Dr. Shaw says that colleagues of his have sometimes kept handicapped children alive against their parents' wishes, only to have parents later be grateful that they did because they decided they wanted the baby after all.[12]

The reason for such ambivalence is simple: parents are shocked by the birth of a handicapped baby, and their emotional state for a time often resembles mourning after a loved one's death. After all, they have lost the healthy, normal baby they had been expecting. They must adjust to the reality of the baby they have been given. Parents in such a position are in no state for mature reflection on the "quality of life" their babies will have.

Most parents eventually adapt to these circumstances, according to Dr. Norman Fost, a pediatrician and professor of the history of medicine at the University of Wisconsin Medical School. They will either take the child into their home or give it over for institutionalization or adoption.

Dr. Fost sensibly recommends that physicians act in a way that facilitates this eventual adaptation. Doctors should clearly, honestly, and repeatedly describe the baby's condition. They need to be willing to listen sympathetically and talk things out. They should encourage parents to see the child and hold it as soon as possible. Above all, they should take medical measures one step at a time. They should not mix urgent decisions about life-sustaining treatment with long-term worries about adoption, custody arrangements, financial burdens, and the effect of a handicapped child on siblings.[13]

The fact is that most parents *do* eventually accept and love their handicapped children. Rosalyn Darling, a medical sociologist, found a revealing pattern in in-depth interviews with the parents of twenty-five children with a variety of serious disabilities, including spina bifida, Down's syndrome, severe cerebral palsy, blindness, and other forms of psycho-motor retardation.[14] Most would not have wanted their child to be born, many wanted it to die in the hospital, but almost all the parents loved their children.

"I can't imagine life without her," said the father of a retarded girl. "The thing I dread most is her death. We know we will lose her someday, and that is the worst thing."

Darling interviewed the parents of a child who was para-lyzed, deformed, and incontinent from spina bifida; they said their daughter brought them great joy. The mother was pregnant at the time of the interview; she would not have an amniocentesis test because she had no intention of aborting an unborn child who might have spina bifida.

These parents did have one complaint: doctors. They complained about doctors who did not want to treat their children and who regarded retarded children as nonpersons. They changed doctors repeatedly and spent much time trying to find doctors who would care for their children humanely and creatively.

When she interviewed physicians, Darling found out why the parents complained. "Most did not welcome such pa-tients," she found. "Several expressed wonder at physicians who devote their entire careers to the treatment of children with severe congenital problems, stating that they could see no rewards in such a practice." One doctor told her: "I can find good things in practically anything—even dying—but birth defects are roaring tragedies. Death doesn't bother me, but the living do."

Doctors who think this way are operating from a new idea of medical ethics. Behind the deed is an attitude and behind the attitude is a philosophy of what is important in life. What is the ethic that lies behind the crime of infanticide?

FIVE

Birth, Death, and the Quality of Life

"It's the same old business of the runt of the litter getting pushed away from the teat."

—James T. Burtchaell

PHYSICIANS WHO ADVOCATE infanticide-on-demand often quote a theologian named Joseph Fletcher.

Fletcher believes that infanticide is acceptable because human beings have a moral obligation to increase human well-being wherever possible. Questions of human rights should not interfere. "All rights are imperfect and can be set aside if human need requires it," he says in one of his essays on human life. Fletcher thinks that man's mastery of technology makes him truly human. "A baby made artificially," he remarks, "by deliberate and careful contrivance, would be more *human* than one resulting from sexual roulette."[1]

Fletcher's views are not unique. Some well-regarded theologians and philosophers hold some disturbing opinions about infanticide.

Bioethicist Peter Singer, in the prestigious medical journal *Pediatrics*: "If we compare a severely defective human infant with a nonhuman animal, a dog or pig, for example, we will often find the nonhuman to have superior capacities, both actual and potential, for rationality, self-consciousness, and anything else that can plausibly be considered morally significant."[2]

Glanville Williams, jurist and moralist at Cambridge University: "An eugenic killing by a mother, exactly parallelled by the bitch that kills her misshapen puppies, cannot confidently be pronounced immoral."[3]

Michael Tooley, professor of philosophy at Stanford University: "The practical moral problem can . . . be satisfactorily handled by choosing some period of time, such as a week after birth, as the interval during which infanticide will be permitted."[4]

Tristram Englehardt, philosopher and physician at the Kennedy Institute, Georgetown University: "[The decision about treatment] belongs properly to the parents because the child belongs to them in a sense that it does not belong to anyone else, even to itself. . . . Clinical and parental judgment may and should be guided by the expected lifestyle and the cost (in parental and societal pain and money) of its attainment."[5]

Author Marvin Kohl: "Beneficent euthanasia is a prima facie obligation. This means that in certain circumstances we have an actual moral obligation to induce death."[6]

A common reaction to such opinions is to dismiss them as grotesque musings by eccentric academics. But they are an important part of the puzzle of infanticide. They have much to do with its growing acceptance. Doctors look to specialists in bioethics for guidance in the treatment of handicapped newborns. So do parents. So do policy-makers and hospital administrators.

Philosophers and theologians sat on a federal government commission that sanctioned experimentation on unborn babies scheduled for abortion, and on a presidential commission that decided in 1983 that stiffer penalties to stop infanticide were not necessary.

A priest-bioethicist helped the American Medical Association formulate "quality of life" criteria to assist doctors deciding when to terminate treatment of handicapped infants. One of his criteria was "potential for human relationships."[7]

Another priest, Fr. John J. Paris, S.J., testified in a murder trial in 1983 that two doctors were morally correct to withdraw food and water from a man only three days after he lapsed into a coma. The man quickly died. Fr. Paris moderated the Ethics Committee Conference of the Concern for Dying Education Council, the successor of the Euthanasia Education Council of America.[8]

In 1973, a Catholic hospital chaplain in Decatur, Illinois, approved the starvation death of a Down's syndrome infant after the parents asked his advice. A priest baptized Infant Doe before his death.

Ethicists also articulate "new" values. Indeed, this is one of the most important reasons why we should pay attention to them and understand what they are saying. The ethics of infanticide in particular has become a frontier where new ideas about human life and human community are being explored and tried out. Ethical issues press urgently in the nursery. What claim do the helpless have on us? What is valuable about human life? What *is* human life? Liberated from Judeo-Christian moral foundations, some ethicists are offering new answers to these old questions—answers which will affect all of us.

The worlds of medicine and bioethics came together in 1974 in Sonoma Valley, California, to begin to offer some of these new answers. The group consisted of an elite collection of twenty participants, nine physicians from medical schools, professors of theology, philosophy, law, social work and other social sciences, and several medical journalists. Their task was to decide what should be done about handicapped infants in the intensive care nursery.[9]

The Sonoma group showed considerable willingness to hasten the deaths of these children. They unanimously agreed that it is sometimes right not to resuscitate an infant at birth and that it is sometimes proper to discontinue life-support. Such decisions could be made if the baby had Down's syndrome, if it was "below human standards for meaningful life," if the infant was likely to be "markedly impaired," if it had "small chance for a normal life," and if it was *unwanted* by its parents and unneeded by society."

Most shocking of all was the group's willingness to kill babies who would not die if left alone. Seventeen of the twenty participants agreed that a self-sustaining baby could be killed in some circumstances. What circumstances? If it had Down's syndrome or other chromosomal disorders, if it was defective and unwanted by parents and society, if it was markedly handicapped and dependent, and if it would have a low "quality of life," it could be killed.

One participant facetiously agreed that a baby in one of these categories could be killed if a judge prepared the fatal syringe, and the parents administered the fatal shot in the presence of "all the lawyers, priests, psychologists, and journalists within a fifty-mile radius and no physicians, nurses, or medical or nursing students were allowed to be present."

The priest-bioethicist who directed the Sonoma panel more seriously concluded that "the morality of active euthanasia is far from settled."

How could a group of eminent physicians and bioethicists reach conclusions so sharply at odds with the classical view that the job of the doctor is to heal, not to kill? It is a reasonable question. The answer is also reasonable in its own way: the Sonoma group viewed human life in a different way. For them, the right of a handicapped baby to treatment and life is carefully hedged. Other values seem to take priority. Indeed, the Sonoma conference participants merely voiced a new scheme of ethics that has come to dominate ethical thinking in the medical profession.

The "new medical ethic" was described in the journal *California Medicine* in 1970.[10] The anonymous editorialist thought that the medical profession was caught between two ethics. The old ethic, nurtured by the Judeo-Christian moral tradition, "placed great emphasis on the intrinsic worth and equal value of every human life regardless of its stage or condition." Opposing it is a "quality of life" ethic that would make it "necessary and acceptable to place relative rather than absolute values on such things as human lives."

What defines a particular individual's "quality of life?" The writer anticipated that the definition would involve the individual's capacity for personal fulfillment, the common welfare, the preservation of the environment, and the betterment of the species.

This writer was prophetic. Babies have in fact been killed for all the reasons he cited: because others think a handicapped infant's life is not worth living, because the burdens of raising handicapped children will interfere with the personal well-being of their parents and siblings, and because disabled people are unproductive and expensive social burdens.

Ethicists give other reasons as well. Some simply do not think that impaired babies are human persons.

Michael Tooley, a philosopher at Stanford University, thinks it unfortunate that most people use the terms "person" and "human being" interchangeably. *Persons* have rights (including a right to life), Tooley says, but not every *human being* can properly be regarded as a *person*. To tell the difference, Tooley lays down a rule: "An organism possesses a serious right to life only if it possesses the concept of a self as a continuing subject of experiences and other mental states, and believes that it is itself such a continuing entity." On this basis, Tooley, would allow infanticide up to a week after birth.

While Tooley disposes of human infants, he worries about animals. Since animals can be self-conscious and conceive of themselves as a continuing entity, they may possess the right to life not accorded to a human infant. Tooley warns: "One may find himself driven to conclude that our everyday treatment of animals is morally indefensible, and that we are in fact murdering innocent persons."[11]

If Tooley doubts the personhood of the handicapped baby, Joseph Fletcher doubts even the child's humanity. Fletcher provides the confused modernist with no less than fifteen criteria to make the critical judgment about whether someone is human. Among them: minimal intelligence, a sense of the future, a sense of the past, a capacity to relate to others, concern for others, and a balance between rationality and feeling. He is vague about what some of these criteria mean, but is specific about others. For example, a human being with an I.Q. of 40 is only questionably a person; below the 20 mark, he is definitely *not* a person.[12]

Some ethicists who write about these issues aren't much concerned about handicapped infants at all. They are apologists for mercy-killing. Disabled newborns are one of several classes of people who they think deserve a speedy and painless death. Their task is to make the naturally repellant idea of killing the helpless a reasonable, even admirable, "option."

Tristram Englehardt, an ethicist who is both a philosopher and a physician, thinks that society must figure out a way to put handicapped children to death. Astoundingly, Englehardt argues that killing is an ethical imperative *from the child's point of view*. A handicapped child, he writes, "has a right not to have its life prolonged."[13]

Others echo Englehardt. "Why should the no-code designation be preferred over the injection?" asks philosopher James Rachels.[14] Some moralists hold that we are sometimes morally compelled to kill. "Beneficent euthanasia is a prima facie obligation," argues Marvin Kohl. "This means that in certain circumstances we have an actual moral obligation to induce death."[15]

These ideas are not confined to scrupulously secular sources. Daniel Maguire, a Catholic theologian teaching at a Catholic university, maintains that it may be moral and should be legal to accelerate the death process by injecting poison or overdosing patients with morphine.[16] (Maguire, of course, does not represent Catholic teaching on this matter.)

Fletcher, like most of these thinkers, is a utilitarian, a man who believes that objective moral norms are irrelevant in determining right and wrong. Rather, the utilitarian believes that the righteous act is the one which brings the greatest good to the greatest number of people.

Fletcher states his guiding principle quite plainly: "Human happiness and well-being is the highest good or *summum bonum*, and . . . therefore any ends or purposes which that ideal or standard validates are just, right, good." Suicide and mercy killing are acceptable in this scheme, as is infanticide. Such acts are not regrettable necessities or grimy compromises with one's conscience, but positive human goods. "It comes down to this," Fletcher writes, "that in some situations a morally good end can justify a relatively 'bad' means."[17]

Many bioethicists today think this way. To speak to them of "rights" and "equality" is to speak a different language.

But the greatest difference is in worldview. The boldest of these bioethicists articulate a new vision of human life which contrasts starkly with the Judeo-Christian value system, which has nourished the West for two thousand years. The first step, says Joseph Fletcher, is to rid ourselves of that obsolete view "according to which God is not only the cause but also the builder of nature and its works, and not only the builder but even the manager."

Theirs is an ethic of human will and power. "It's the same old business of the runt of the litter getting pushed away from the teat," says theologian James Burtchaell.

Marvin Kohl, for example, thinks mercy-killing advances human dignity, if dignity is understood in Kohl's special sense as something synonomous with one's ability to control his own life. In order to assert his dignity, a man might want to kill himself, or have himself killed if he is comatose or bedridden because then he is no longer in control. We can kill such a person mercifully, says Kohl, in respect for his "dignity."[18]

Tristram Englehardt believes that we have moral duties not to give existence to other persons (and to take existence from them) precisely because it is in our power to do so. "Humans can now control reproduction," he writes. "One must now decide when and under what circumstances persons will come into existence." For Englehardt, deciding whether to let a handicapped newborn live is simply one aspect of birth control.[19]

Joseph Fletcher describes the clash of value systems most starkly. On the one hand is a "simplistic" view which holds that "living and dying are in God's hands and that life is God's to give and only God's to take." On the other is "humanistic medicine," with its ethic of responsibility, including "responsibility for the termination of subhuman life in posthuman beings."[20]

Such is the noxious moral climate in which infanticide has flourished. One important issue we confront is whether this ethical climate can change. The issue is not *whether* certain values and vision will be imposed on American life, but *whose* values will be reflected in our law and public policy. A materialistic, utilitarian, cost/benefit, secular vision is now aggressively ascendent.

The struggle is over conflicting ideas about what it means to be human and what it takes to live in human community. The ethicists who would rationalize infanticide are elitists. To be "human" in their definition would require men and women to be more than merely human. They shroud their intentions in euphemisms and frame their criteria for death in such elusively subjective terms that their ethics are really anti-ethics. They attack the foundations of human community. They pretend that man's dark side does not exist.

The truth is that a disabled baby struggling for life is a human being. Most of us, despite the efforts of situation ethicists and radical utilitarians, are still able to recognize that this is so. Despite sickness or handicaps or probable social circumstances in later life, the disabled child is one of us, a creature of God, a pearl of great price. We should take comfort from this recognition, for here is a source of hope that man's dark side will not prevail.

SIX

Hard Cases and Hard Questions

"The easiest solution is simply to do everything technology allows: plug the kid in."
— Rev. John J. Paris, S.J.

T HE BIOETHICISTS WE HAVE HEARD from in the last chapter are good at getting our attention. We sit up and take note when we hear handicapped infants described as subhuman organisms devoid of rights. We have much to worry about when such views get a respectful hearing in reputable publications.

It is hard to avoid the impression that some physicians *use* certain bioethicists as apologists for their actions. For their part, certain bioethicists virtually become intellectual accessories to murder.

Yet there are some genuine ethical questions to ask about the care of handicapped infants. Do bioethicists have anything to say about the standard for making treatment decisions? Does modern medical technology present new ethical problems? How does one decide whether a possible course of treatment is not morally required?

Ethicists more subtle than Fletcher and Tooley have exercised great influence on medical thinking about questions like these. But many of their answers have been equally unsatisfactory. In fact, their work may be even more corrosive precisely because they exercise such great influence.

The influence of bioethicists on the practice of medicine in the intensive care nursery was formally noted in 1981 when the American Medical Association issued a new guideline for the treatment of handicapped infants. It was entitled "Quality of Life." This is what it advised physicians to do:

> In caring for defective infants, the advice and judgment of the physician should be readily available but the decision whether to treat a severely defective infant and exert maximal efforts to sustain life should be the choice of the parents. The parents should be told the options, expected benefits, risks, and limits of any proposed care, *how the potential for human relationships is affected by the infant's condition* and relevant information and answers to their questions.[1] (Emphasis added.)

This guideline disturbed many physicians. The tone of it seemed to be weighted against the baby; it seemed to presume that a decision to let the child die was forthcoming. The guideline also ascribed no moral worth to the child. Whatever value he or she had derived from the opinions of others. Many physicians deplored the lack of a clear statement of the traditional view that pediatricians should be advocates for children in trouble. Others thought its description of the decision-making process was fanciful. Physicians, they said, have more influence over treatment decisions than parents do, and it is mischievous to pretend otherwise.

But perhaps the most curious feature of the guideline was a phrase towards the end: "how the potential for human relationships is affected by the infant's condition." This has become known as "the relational principle." It was a vague phrase, subject to endless subjective interpretations, quite out of place in a medical statement. The relational principle does not, in fact, come from a medical source at all. It was the product of the most influential of the bioethicists who have addressed these issues—a Jesuit priest named Richard McCormick.

Unlike some ethicists we have heard from, Fr. McCormick reasons lucidly and carefully, makes no outrageous statements, and mounts no assault on traditional ethics. Indeed, he starts from the most traditional ethical authority of all—the Christian scriptures. As a Christian he believes that men were created to serve higher purposes: to love God and to love their neighbor—two loves that are inseparable. He quotes 1 John 4:20-21: "If any man says I love God and hates his brother, he is a liar. For he who loves not his brother, whom he sees, how can he love God whom he does not see?"

From this, Fr. McCormick draws some striking conclusions.

"It is in others that God demands to be recognized and loved," he says. "If this is true, it means that, in Judeo-Christian perspective, the meaning, substance and consummation of life is found in human *relationships*, and the qualities of justice, respect, concern, compassion, and support that surround them."[2]

Writing in the *Journal of the American Medical Association*, one of the most influential medical journals in America, Fr. McCormick lays down a relational principle for handicapped newborns.

A life that is "painful, poverty-stricken and deprived, away from home and friends, oppressive," might well be a life of which it could be said that "human relationships—which are the very possibility of growth in love of God and neighbor—would be so threatened, strained or submerged that they would no longer function as the heart and meaning of the individual's life as they should." In such cases, the Christian can say that life has achieved its potential, and the individual can be allowed to die. This guideline, he hopes, "may help in decisions about sustaining the lives of grossly deformed and deprived infants."

Grossly deformed and deprived? What does that mean? How indeed can healthy adults with no experience of disability imagine the quality and value of relationships a handicapped baby might have in future years?

Fr. McCormick is not insensitive to the difficulty of answering such questions, but he unhelpfully places the burden of proof on the infant. He approves a surgeon's opinion that "if a severely handicapped child were suddenly given one moment of omniscience and total awareness of his or her outlook for the future, would that child necessarily opt for life? No one has yet been able to demonstrate that the answer would always be 'yes.' "

Of course no one can demonstrate that; it's an entirely speculative question, and Fr. McCormick may well be right to say that some infants would choose to die "in some instances."[3] The question is: in what instances?

There is another question: would it make any moral difference if Fr. McCormick or anyone else could identify such infants? The prospect of a medical ethic that permits killing people because they do not want to live is hardly appealing.

The fact is that the relational principle is deficient in practice as well as in theory. People will always draw the line about relationships in different places.

For example, what about an Infant Doe: a baby with an irreparable chromosomal disorder, a correctible but life-threatening complication, and parents who are convinced that the child's relational capacity will be substandard? How can the relational principle insist that he have surgery if the operation will do nothing to improve his capacity for relationships?

Whether these relationships will be substandard is simply a matter of opinion. Fr. McCormick would demand the operation. He was harsh on the authorities responsible for the

Infant Doe case, calling it "nothing less than a state-authored deprivation of innocent life without either due process of law or the equal protection of the laws."[4] As infanticide has become more common, he has issued many cautions: babies should not die because their families cannot cope with them; retarded babies should not be left to starve because they are retarded; nontreatment decisions are not private matters as doctors claim; the courts can properly intervene when decision-makers behave irresponsibly.[5]

But nothing in the relational principle compels anyone to agree with Fr. McCormick about any of this.

As Dennis Horan, a lawyer and co-editor of *Death, Dying, and Euthanasia,* points out, "there is no way that this relational principle can be less than a death warrant for some retardates except in the hands of Fr. McCormick himself."[6] But the problem is deeper than that. The relational principle is no principle at all. It falls apart as soon as one begins to apply it to specific cases.

It is worth trying to understand how Fr. McCormick went wrong in his ethical reasoning. One of his mistakes was to focus too narrowly on so-called hard cases—those rare situations where the infant's disabilities are truly severe and the medical prognosis genuinely perplexing. We often think about hard cases when we consider these problems, and doctors who want to ease handicapped babies into death often emphasize the plight of those who are in the worst condition.

Lawyers have a wise saying: "hard cases make bad law." They mean that laws made to deal with bizarre, unusual, or extreme cases are often irrelevant or even unjust when applied to more common situations. Ethicists who lay down rules for letting handicapped newborns die should heed this aphorism.

Fr. McCormick concentrates on hard cases in the intensive care nursery and he describes them in highly emotive language. They are infants whose lives can be sustained, "but in a wretched, painful, or deformed condition," babies who might have "a terribly mutilated body from birth," or face "a life that is from birth one long, painful, oppressive convalescence."[7]

Who are these babies? Fr. McCormick describes them in these infinitely tragic terms:

> In neonatal intensive care units . . . we are dealing with tiny patients who have no history, have had no chance at life, and have no say in the momentous decision about their treatment. Some are born with anomalies or birth accidents so utterly devastating (especially extensive brain damage) that they will never rise much above the "persistent vegetative state."[8]

It is seriously misleading to suggest that babies like these are the typical patients in neonatal intensive care units. These "tiny patients" do exist—at least for a brief period—and deciding whether and how to treat them can be genuinely difficult. There can be some superficial plausibility in considering the capacity for relationships of an infant so badly damaged that it will not be able to interact with the world in any way. Yet a relational principle formulated for them should not be applied to most of the eighty-two or so handicapped infants born in the U.S. each day.

Fr. McCormick's description of these hard cases is full of sincere concern that the lives of these infants will be burdensome to them. Yet the problem is different. The plain truth is that the infants who become targets for what is properly termed infanticide are those whose handicaps make them burdens for *others*, not for themselves.

Very severely disabled infants are born. But we should not look to them as the starting point for ethical principles to guide treatment of all handicapped children.

Fr. McCormick and other bioethicists who would introduce "quality of life" considerations into neonatal treatment decisions make other unsound assumptions as well. Two key themes run through their thinking. One is opposition to what they call "vitalism." Joseph Fletcher defines vitalism as the proposition that "we are always obliged to prolong life as much as possible."[9] The second theme is great distress over the effect of medical technology. The ethical dilemmas in the nursery, these ethicists say, are caused by the new ability of physicians to rescue babies who would have died in years past.

Both notions deserve the most careful scrutiny.

Fr. John J. Paris, a theologian and sometime collaborator with Fr. McCormick, rejects vitalism on religious grounds. It is idolatry, he says, to view death as an unmitigated evil and life as an absolute good. Vitalism makes life "an end and a goal in itself, a new golden calf before which we may worship."[10]

Advanced medical technology, moreover, has given vitalists dangerous tools, he says. Seriously handicapped and diseased babies died swiftly in years past because nothing could be done for them. Things are different now. We face entirely new ethical problems. Fr. Paris says that the ethical task is to stop modern doctors from using technological tools to preserve every life they possibly can, regardless of the patient's prospects. "When the difficult questions concerning the appropriate care of defective neonates arise," he says, "the easiest solution is simply to do everything technology allows: plug the kid in. That way, one is absolved from having to make difficult decisions."[11]

Fr. Paris advances the remarkable proposition that the prolife movement is to blame for these problems. Prolifers, he argues, have successfully pressured medical people into agreeing "that life is ultimate and that everything possible must be done to sustain it." The result? Prolifers "are responsible for creating disastrous coma ward situations in this country which will soon become so abhorrent that there will be a public outcry to stop the madness by actively terminating the lives of such victims of our technology."

What is to be done? Fr. McCormick and Fr. Paris would establish broad guidelines to allow physicians and parents to make "quality of life" judgments about handicapped infants.[12]

But is this an accurate picture of the problem in the intensive care nursery?

Let us first look at the philosophical issue—the hypothesis that "vitalism" dominates the thinking of physicians.

A rigid insistence that biological life must be prolonged at all costs has never been a part of good medical care. Doctors and nurses deal with dying patients all the time. They continually make *medical* judgments about whether therapies will be useful. When further treatment is pointless, doctors will usually cease life-sustaining efforts and allow a patient to die peacefully. As ethicist Paul Ramsey says, those caring for the dying "need only to be sensitive and apt to determine when attempts to cure or save life are no longer indicated—that is, when in place of any longer bothering the dying with vain treatments, the indicated medical care calls upon us to surround them instead with a human presence while they die."[13]

It would be hard to find a good physician who would disagree with that statement and conduct his care of the dying in any other way. Of course, it can be difficult to decide when someone is in the process of dying. Family members can insist that doctors "do everything" when the right medical decision may be to let the individual die. But few doctors favor this approach. To the contrary, most deplore it. There is certainly no evidence that the problem is so serious that we must replace medical judgments with subjective "quality of life" guidelines to decide when people should die.

Indeed, vitalism is irrelevant to the issue of infanticide. Once again we must make the point that the babies who are targets for infanticide are not dying. The lives of Infant Doe and Baby Jane Doe, Phillip Becker, the Hopkins baby, and the other infants we have met in this book were taken or threatened for *social reasons* —not because of their medical condition.

What about technology, Fr. Paris's "disasterous coma ward

situations" where doctors automatically "plug the kid in?"

Technology is also a largely irrelevant issue in infanticide for the same reasons that the charge of "vitalism" misses the point. Desperate and mistaken attempts to save life at all costs are decidedly *not* problems at Yale-New Haven, Johns Hopkins, and Bloomington Hospitals—at least with certain newborn infants. Infant Doe and his fellow victims died because medical technology that would have been applied to "normal" babies was *not* made available to them.

But concern about medical technology is not completely beside the point here. In fact, we are concerned about infanticide in large part because new medical technology allows physicians to rescue many *more* seriously ill newborns today than they could twenty years ago. Almost all spina bifida infants would have died before 1960. Today almost all can be saved. Very tiny premature infants who would invariably have died in the past can now be sustained in modern neonatal intensive care units.

As a result, doctors will face the question of whether to save a handicapped baby more frequently today than in the past.

But are the ethical issues involved in the decision of *whether* to use such technology really different from what they have always been? A physician today ponders whether to recommend a low-risk but recently perfected operation to close the hole in a spina bifida child's spine. Forty years ago he might have wondered whether it was worth using newly-developed antibiotics to treat the same child's meningitis. In both cases, he may face the temptation to let the child die for "quality of life" reasons—for some reason other than a medical indication. As one professor of pediatrics comments, "neonatology has always had its ethical problems."[14]

It is doubtful whether medical technology has created *new* ethical problems in the intensive care nursery, though it has created *more* of them. Technology forces physicians to ask the ethical questions more frequently and insistently. The questions still need to be answered. The increasing popularity of "nontreatment" is caused more by an erosion in ethics than by an escalation in technology.

Fr. McCormick and Fr. Paris claim that the guidance they offer about the treatment of handicapped newborns draws on the classic moral distinction between "ordinary" and "extraordinary" means of treatment. This concept was developed by Catholic theologians to help people judge when medical treatment imposed excessive burdens and could rightly be withheld.

Many ethicists argue that life-saving treatment of handicapped newborns is often "extraordinary" and thus not morally required. Some do not claim to speak from an avowedly Christian viewpoint, but seem to adopt this "Catholic" idea to lend a veneer of religious authority to a radically utilitarian view. But Christian thinkers like Fr. Paris and Fr. McCormick also use this distinction to justify withholding treatment from disabled infants. And it is a curious fact that many of the parents involved in such cases have been Catholics, and they often claim church sanction for their decisions to let their handicapped babies die.[15]

The distinction between ordinary and extraordinary means is a commonsensical idea: no one is morally obliged to use all conceivable treatments to preserve his life, but only those treatments that offer a reasonable hope of success and do not impose excessive burdens. A person with a brain tumor is not obliged to have an operation that might save his life but leave him with severe mental impairment. A terminally ill heart patient can morally choose to die rather than undergo experimental heart surgery. On the other hand, a blood transfusion for an accident victim or an operation that has a good chance of excising a malignant tumor are usually classified as ordinary treatment. Patients should submit to them out of respect for their own lives (and often for the sake of loved ones). Those who make medical decisions on others' behalf—parents of minor children, for example—are under the same obligation.

What is an extraordinary treatment? The U.S. Catholic bishops have laid down two criteria: treatment which offers no reasonable hope of recovery and treatment that imposes excessive burdens on the patient and perhaps also on his family.[16]

It is clearly an abuse of this idea to claim, as some ethicists have, that surgery to repair an esophageal fistula (Infant Doe) or to close an open spine in a spina bifida infant (Baby Jane Doe) are excessively burdensome medical procedures. "Burdensome" in this branch of Catholic theology refers to the anticipated impact of the treatment *on the patient*. The infanticide ethicists would twist this to mean that the *success* of surgery would be burdensome *to the families* because it preserves the life of an infant the parents do not want.

Some ethicists argue that such treatment is excessively burdensome because it inflicts a burdensome life on the child. But this suggests that life with physical and mental impairments is an inferior life. Such a belief is rooted in prejudice against handicapped people.

Some ethicists also argue that operations like those denied Infant Doe are "extraordinary" because the patient will still be handicapped even after a successful operation. But "reasonable benefit" refers to the probability that the medical treatment will accomplish its purpose. It may not solve all the patient's medical problems, but it is not ethically extraordinary if it will solve some of them for a patient who is not dying.[17]

The truth is that the distinction between ordinary and extraordinary means is intended to answer difficult medical questions at the end of life—not the beginning. It is for the gravely ill or critically injured patient who must weigh the burdens and benefits of a proposed treatment that may not cure him, may well hurt him, and would burden his family besides. A serious medical condition—cancer, heart disease, an accident—has made his condition terminal. The treatment is "extraordinary" because it won't do much for him.

The situation is almost exactly reversed for the handicapped newborn. The treatment is called "extraordinary" because it *will* help. It is the decision not to treat that makes his condition terminal. A nonmedical factor—his projected I.Q., a doctor's ideas about meaningful life, his parents' aspirations—make him unwanted. Social reasons, not medical indications, make his treatment "extraordinary."

The issue, in other words, is not whether dying infants should have high-risk, painful operations. No one believes they should. Rather, the ethical issue we are concerned with is whether handicapped infants should receive the same treatment non-handicapped infants receive.

That, as we shall see next, is the legal issue as well.

SEVEN

From the Delivery Room to the Courtroom

"Although the law clothes the defective infant with a right to life, many people think that right ends when it conflicts with the interests of parents, the medical profession, and the infant's own potential for full development."

—John A. Robertson

JEFF AND SCOTT MUELLER were born May 6, 1981 at Lakeview Medical Center in Danville, Illinois. Their parents were well known at the hospital: Dr. Robert Mueller was head of the emergency room staff, and Pamela Mueller worked at Lakeview as a nurse.

The Muellers had known for some time that they were expecting twins: an extra doctor was on hand to help out with the delivery. They did not know that Jeff and Scott would be Siamese twins, joined at the waist, sharing one of their three legs.

In the minutes following birth, a decision concerning the twins' treatment was reached among the Muellers and the physicians. The order, "Do not feed in accordance with parents' wishes," was written on their medical chart. Jeff and Scott were taken to the newborn nursery to die.

But they did not die. At least one of the nurses on the floor could not bear to witness the deliberate starvation of the two babies, and defied the doctors' orders by giving them food and water surreptitiously.

On May 13, a week after the twins' birth, an anonymous phone caller alerted the Illinois Department of Children and Family Services to what was going on at Lakeview. A social worker went to the hospital to investigate, and on May 15 the department charged the parents with neglect and asked for temporary custody of the children. A court granted the request and Family Services transferred Jeff and Scott to prestigious Children's Memorial Hospital in Chicago.

A month later, on June 11, the district attorney for Vermilion County—the county in which the twins had been born—took the unprecedented step of charging the parents and the attending physician with conspiracy to commit murder and with endangering the life and health of children. A preliminary hearing to determine the validity of the charges was held on July 17. Several nurses testified, but they were either unable or unwilling to definitely link the doctor or the parents with the order to withhold food. The judge dismissed the charges due to insufficient evidence.[1]

The story of the Danville twins resembles others we have seen, but it has a unique significance. For one thing, it has a relatively happy ending: Jeff and Scott were successfully separated by surgeons at Children's Memorial and, when the state dropped its neglect charges against their parents, were returned home.

But more than this, the Danville case marked the first time that criminal charges were brought against parents and doctors for withholding food, water, and routine medical treatment from a handicapped newborn.[2] The story of Jeff and Scott Mueller graphically illustrates the problems involved in trying to move infanticide from the delivery room to the courtroom.

Why doesn't infanticide get into court? The almost complete absence of legal activity is one of the more puzzling aspects of the infanticide problem. People hearing the story of Infant Doe for the first time often ask, incredulously, "But isn't that murder?" It certainly *looks* like murder. Indeed, dozens of similar cases of infanticide have come to light over the past decade. Details of many of these cases have become widely known, and suggest that grounds for prosecution do exist.

Yet authorities have been extremely reluctant to get involved. The Danville case remains the only instance in which criminal charges have ever been filed; no convictions have ever been obtained. Indeed, some observers suggest that infanticide persists, in part, because the conspicuous absence of prosecution creates the impression that the law allows it.[3]

This absence of legal activity seems especially odd in a society that is not exactly shy about resolving problems through the courts. What accounts for it? Is it not against the law to deny life-saving surgery to infants merely because they are mentally or physically handicapped? Is it not illegal to starve such babies to death?

Indeed it *is* illegal. That, perhaps, is one of the most important points to be emphasized. The duties of medical professionals toward their patients, and of parents toward their children, are grounded not only in sentiment or tradition or professional ethics; they are also grounded in law. A review of the legal literature yields a rather imposing catalogue of those duties, and of the criminal and civil liabilities that may be incurred by those who fail to meet them.

First, consider the parents. The law imposes on them the duty to care for their children and to protect them from harm, a duty which certainly includes the obligation to seek out appropriate medical care when their children need it. Dr. John A. Robertson, who teaches law and medicine at the University of Wisconsin, summarizes the parents' situation:

Every state imposes on parents a legal duty to provide necessary medical assistance to a helpless minor child. If they withhold such care and the child dies, they may be prosecuted for manslaughter or murder, as has frequently occurred when parents have refused or neglected to obtain medical care for nondefective children. . . . In addition to homicide, parents may also be liable under statutes that make it criminal for a parent to neglect to support or to provide necessities, to fail to furnish medical attention, to maltreat, to be cruel to, or to endanger the child's life or health.[4]

The duties and liabilities of the physician are no less exacting. When a doctor agrees to care for an individual, in the eyes of the law he has established a contract with that patient. That contractual relationship imposes a number of obligations on him which remain in force so long as the doctor-patient relationship remains in existence. If the doctor fails to meet these obligations, he could be in serious trouble. Dr. Robertson:

> The physician who has contracted with the parents to deliver and treat their newborn infant has assumed an obligation to act on the infant's behalf. . . . The attending physician who withholds lifesaving treatment from a defective infant may be found culpable of homicide. . . .[5]

However, the decision to let handicapped babies die is usually the parents,' at least nominally. If the parents *instruct* the physician to withhold treatment from their infant, does this not terminate the doctor-patient relationship and relieve the physician of criminal liability for homicide?

Robertson, among others, does not think so. He does not believe that the doctor-patient relationship normally can be terminated in this way. Even if it could, he says, a doctor who cooperates with a parental decision to commit murder can still be found guilty of homicide "if his actions make him an accessory-before-the-fact to a homicide by the parents."[6]

A physician who participates in a decision to withhold treatment may also be charged with violation of state child neglect laws, failure to notify authorities of child neglect and abuse, and even conspiracy to commit murder.[7]

Nor are doctors the only ones who can get into legal trouble. Hospitals are generally held responsible to oversee the care provided to their patients; hence hospital administrators risk criminal liabilities if infanticide occurs in their facility.[8] Nurses, too, could be charged with crimes ranging from homicide to conspiracy, though the nurse's subordinate relationship to the physician complicates the question somewhat.[9]

All these parties—doctors, nurses, hospital administrators—can also be sued under civil law. Parents can sue them for neglect of duty, malpractice, or wrongful death if the parents felt they were induced to make a decision to withhold care based on inaccurate or misleading medical advice.[10]

Finally, medical professionals can have their licenses revoked and be disciplined in other ways by state licensing boards for actions deemed to constitute professional incompetency, gross negligence, or departure from ordinary standards of care, whether or not those actions resulted in prosecutions or lawsuits.[11]

Homicide. Manslaughter. Child Neglect. Conspiracy. Malpractice. These crimes certainly seem to have occurred in many of the cases we have considered in this book. Yet prosecutions rarely occur. Why?

The most obvious reason is that infanticide is almost always a secret crime. Prosecutors do not bring charges because they do not know that a crime has taken place.

"If a child is going to be starved to death in a hospital," observes Dr. Koop, "it is usually a fairly tight secret among a small group of people. If someone is committing homicide he doesn't usually announce it from the rooftops."[12]

Case histories bear this out. Decisions to withhold food, water, and medical care from handicapped infants are usually made quietly and discreetly among physicians and parents. The decisions are usually carried out with a minimum of fanfare so as not to attract undue attention from other hospital personnel. When instances of suspected infanticide do come to light, it is usually because someone familiar with the incident, but not involved in making the original decison, has notified authorities. This was the case in Danville and in Bloomington.

The informants have almost always been nurses who resist doctors' orders to withhold care. Dr. Koop has said that in his first two years as Surgeon General he received more than twenty phone calls from nurses who were aware of apparent cases of infanticide-in-progress and didn't know what to do about them.[13]

One result of all this, of course, is to draw the shroud of secrecy even tighter around nontreatment decisions. One law journal article cautions about the inevitable presence of "snoopy hospital personnel" and "do-gooders" who might interfere with an otherwise private decision.[14]

However, even when a case of suspected infanticide *is* reported, chances are that no charges will be filed.

Prosecutors do not like such cases. Prosecutions entailing medical issues tend to be complex, requiring a high level of technical knowledge on the part of the attorney, and often involving confusing (if not contradictory) expert testimony. To prosecute a physician for his handling of a particular patient is, in effect, to second-guess professional medical judgments. Some crucial elements of fact may be impossible to obtain, and some crucial elements of interpretation impossible to reconstruct outside the original clinical situation. This is what happened in the Danville case; the judge dismissed charges when one crucial link in the evidence could not be substantiated.

Faced with a situation of such potential complexity, a hard-pressed district attorney may well conclude that he lacks adequate time, money, and expertise to prosecute an infanticide case.

State child protective service agencies, which have shown reluctance to get involved in some Baby Doe cases, tend to feel the same way. As one government official told the authors, "If you go visit your local child-abuse agency, what you're likely to find is two or three social workers crammed into a tiny office and buried under a mountain of manila folders. It's not their fault, but they just haven't got what they need to do the job."

All those hindrances might be overcome if prosecutors and state authorities *wanted* to prosecute cases of suspected infanticide. The fact is, however, that they frequently do not.

The reasons are many. The prosecutor may agree with the nontreatment decision. He may see the issue simply as one of professional judgment and parental prerogative, and in effect "delegate" the authority to settle a sticky problem to doctors and parents.[15] This is what the courts did in the Bloomington Infant Doe case, where the "medical treatment" selected by the parents was deliberate starvation of their child.

Mainly, however, prosecutors and other authorities shy away from infanticide cases because they tend to be unpopular and politically dangerous.

The local prosecutor, more than any other official, sets the law enforcement agenda for the community. By aggressively prosecuting various categories of crimes and declining to prosecute others, he tells the police and the community what is important and what can be tolerated.

This agenda-setting is necessary. Law enforcement should reflect local concerns; a prosecutor must prioritize his concerns in order to match his limited resources to the needs of his community.

But the process can also be political. District attorneys are elected officials. If they are to remain in office, they must be responsive both to public sentiment and to the interests of influential segments of the community.

Among these influential segments is the local medical establishment. As syndicated columnist George F. Will told a television interviewer, "Doctors, whatever else is true about them, are pillars of their communities. And prosecutors don't tangle with pillars of the community if they can avoid it."[16]

But beyond this, infanticide cases tend to be controversial and unpopular with the public at large. James Bopp, Jr, general counsel for the National Right to Life Committee, notes that "even though mercy-killing is prohibited by homicide statutes, the practice is seldom punished, and the few prosecutions that have occurred have resulted in a large number of sentimental acquittals, suspended sentences, or reprieves." He cites a typical case in which "an outcry of public opinion favored the mercy-killer."[17]

Indeed, the public often perceives infanticide as a form of mercy-killing. Remember Daniel McKay, the veterinarian charged with homicide after reportedly bashing his handicapped son's head against the floor moments after the baby's birth. A reporter who visited Harvey some months later was surprised to find that residents of what he described as "a deeply religious community" seemed to sympathize with Dr. McKay. Many spoke philosophically of "reaching the breaking point," and wondered whether they would not have reacted similarly under the circumstances.[18] Would a jury of Harvey citizens convict Daniel McKay for his appalling actions?

In view of the many legal, logistical, attitudinal, and political impediments, it is not surprising that the actual liability of parents, physicians, and others involved in non-treatment decisions is considerably less than a review of the statute books might seem to suggest. Infanticide prosecutions have not been plentiful and, under such conditions, are not likely to be.

Just how prominent a role *should* criminal prosecution play as a weapon against infanticide? There are sound reasons why this kind of legal action should not be viewed as a main line of attack. As one legal scholar has observed, "Case by case litigation of newborn treatment decisions will be expensive, time-consuming, and complicated, and can lead to inconsistent results."[19] Also, a judicial proceeding which operates according to formal legal rules is not always the best forum for airing the moral and theological issues surrounding infanticide.

However, prosecution can have great deterrent value in cases where the important issues can be clearly drawn. Professor Robertson suggests that publicity concerning Baby Doe cases may well lead to more prosecutions in the future, which in turn will cause doctors and parents to take second thought before deciding to withhold routine care from a handicapped newborn.[20]

Even so, he cautions, the strategy can backfire:

Prosecution, if it occurs at all, should be a last resort, reserved for the most flagrant cases where the violation of rights is clearest. Ill-considered prosecutions will only lead to acquittals, and to a commuity backlash that could lead ultimately to even less respect for the rights of the handicapped.[21]

What then? Handicapped newborns are citizens of the United States, and fully covered by the Fourteenth Amendment's guarantee of equal protection under the law. Indeed, given his inability to speak for himself, and the apparent readiness of parents and physicians to overlook his rights, the handicapped newborn needs more legal protection than the rest of us, not less. Where is it to come from?

We will consider this question from a number of angles later. In the meantime, as Robertson points out, the questions raised by the legal aspects of infanticide point to whole new areas of concern.

"Although the law clothes the defective infant with a right

to life," he says, "many people think that right ends when it conflicts with the interests of parents, the medical profession, and the infant's own potential for full development."[22]

Are the infant's rights limited? Let us look at a case in which the questions of competing rights and interests played a prominent and controversial role.

EIGHT

In the Matter of Baby Jane Doe

"This poor baby girl is truly alone in the world."
—Attorney William Weber,
guardian for Baby Jane Doe,

D AN AND LINDA A. had been married only a few months
when they learned that Linda was pregnant.

The young couple was delighted, and made happy prepara-
tions. Dan, a building contractor, had two new rooms built
onto their brick-and-shingle ranch house in Suffolk County,
New York, and decorated one of them as a nursery.

The baby was due in late September, but Linda's due date
came and went. After three weeks her doctor, concerned by the
delay and by the baby's apparently erratic heartbeat, recommended an emergency delivery by Caesarean section. The baby
was born at 10:22 A.M., Tuesday, October 11, 1983, at St.
Charles Hospital in Port Jefferson, New York.

The shock of the unexpected surgery was bad enough,
Linda would say later, but a worse shock awaited her. Linda
said she first suspected something was wrong when the
doctors put her under general anesthesia immediately after the
delivery.

"They told me I had a baby girl," Linda recalled, "and I

started to cry. I wanted to hold her. That was what was supposed to happen. But they said no. And then they put me to sleep."

When Linda awoke, Dan told her that their newborn daughter was tragically handicapped. Dan had been present in the operating room during the delivery. As his baby girl had come into the world, he had immediately noticed "the sac on her back," indicating a disability known as spina bifida, or incomplete closure of the spinal column.

There were other complications as well. The baby had hydrocephalus, or excess fluid on the brain, not uncommon in spina bifida babies. In addition, she appeared to have microcephaly, or an undersized head. (This diagnosis would later be disputed.)

Dan spent several hours that day talking to doctors about his daughter's future treatment.

Dr. Arjen Keuskamp, a neurologist at St. Charles Hospital, recommended that corrective surgery be performed as soon as possible. Dan seemed to agree. At about six o'clock that evening, the infant was transferred to the better-equipped University Hospital, at the State University of New York at Stony Brook. Dan signed the baby's admission papers, as well as a form giving consent for anesthesia to be administered.

But sometime in the next few hours, Dan changed his mind. There were more consultations, with doctors, nurses, relatives, clergy. Among the doctors was George Newman, a pediatric neurologist at Stony Brook, who examined the baby and gave Dan his prognosis—one that differed markedly from Dr. Keuskamp's. At 11:30 that night, after talking to Dr. Newman, Dan decided to withdraw consent to surgery for his daughter. Linda later concurred in his decision. Dr. Keuskamp did not, and resigned from the case in protest.

In the days that followed, Dan and Linda visited their daughter in Stony Brook's intensive care nursery.

"I brought booties to the hospital for her, white with faces on them, pale colored shirts," Linda said. "I decided to bring some clothes and make it nice for her."

The hardest part, they said, was going home each day without their daughter. "The crib and cradle were all set up," Linda said, "and the clothes are in the drawers. We were just so excited about having this baby. Then this tragedy occurred."

On each visit, Dan and Linda held their baby, fed her, changed her diapers, adjusted the gauze bandages on the lesion in her spine. They spoke to her, calling her by name. For many months, only they knew what that name was: to the rest of the world she was known simply as Baby Jane Doe.[1]

Was the decision not to operate on Baby Jane Doe—the decision reached during those late-night discussions at University Hospital—an appropriate one, given Jane Doe's condition and prognosis?

That was what Lawrence Washburn wanted to know.

Washburn had never met Jane Doe or her parents. He was an attorney from Vermont, an activist who had handled a number of right-to-life cases. He was also the father of a handicapped thirteen-year-old daughter.

On Friday, October 14, three days after Baby Jane Doe's birth, Washburn, acting on a confidential tip, filed a petition asking a judge to appoint a special guardian for the infant, and to order corrective surgery performed at once.

Washburn thought the issues in the case were clear. He sympathized with the parents, but was more concerned with the rights of Baby Jane Doe herself. He thought she might not be getting the treatment she deserved because of her handicap.[2]

The judge, State Supreme Court Justice Melvyn Tanenbaum, agreed. On Wednesday, October 20, he ordered the hospital to operate on the nine-day-old infant and appointed New York attorney William Weber as her guardian *ad litem*, meaning he was empowered to represent the infant's legal interests in court. Washburn, his task completed, bowed out of the case.[3]

But his victory was short-lived. Two days later, on Friday, October 21, the state Supreme Court's Appellate Division reversed Tanenbaum's ruling.[4]

William Weber, the court-appointed guardian, pressed on. The next Monday, October 24, he asked New York State's highest tribunal, the Court of Appeals, to compel the hospital to perform corrective surgery on the now thirteen-day-old infant.

Weber, like Washburn, presented the case as a question of the limits of parental authority. Parents have a right to make decisions for their children, he told the court. "But that right is not so broad that it gives them the freedom to bring about their children's death by deliberate medical neglect. Parents may not rely on the Constitution to inflict serious harm on their children."[5]

On Friday, October 28, the Court of Appeals turned Weber down. It issued a unanimous and strongly-worded endorsement of the parents' right to be the final arbiters of the type of medical care Jane Doe would receive. The court reserved its harshest language for Lawrence Washburn, the man who had brought the case to court. The court condemned "the unusual, and sometimes offensive, activities of those who have sought, in the interests of Baby Jane Doe, to displace parental responsibility for, and management of, her medical care."[6]

Weber later decided to try one last time. He asked the U.S. Supreme Court to review the Court of Appeals ruling. "This poor baby girl is truly alone in the world," Weber's written brief said. But the Court declined to hear the appeal.[7]

By November, the legal effort to save Jane Doe, begun by Lawrence Washburn and continued by William Weber, had reached a dead end.

But already a new initiative was underway on another front, one that would transform the case of Baby Jane Doe into a nationwide controversy. Even as the state court proceedings were still in progress, the federal government had entered the picture.

On October 19, the Department of Health and Human Services' Office for Civil Rights (OCR) received a call on its twenty-four-hour Baby Doe telephone line complaining that Jane Doe was being denied proper medical care because of her handicaps.

OCR referred the complaint to the New York State Child Protection Service, the agency responsible for investigating suspected incidents of child abuse and neglect. The agency took no action, and it later reported it had found no cause for state intervention on Jane Doe's behalf.[8]

In the meantime, OCR had received copies of medical records for the first eight days of Jane Doe's life. The office called Stony Brook to ask for the rest of the records. The hospital refused. The government repeated its request. The hospital repeated its refusal.

Dr. Koop, sensing the looming confrontation, was pursuing some behind-the-scenes involvement. Through a mutual friend, he tried to make contact with Jane Doe's doctors. His aim was to talk with them as a fellow physician, not in his official capacity, and urge them to seek a second opinion about Jane Doe's treatment. This, he hoped, would forstall a wider controversy and serve the infant's interests more directly. But his attempts at private intervention did not succeed.

Frustrated by the hospital's lack of cooperation, the Department of Health and Human Services (HHS) turned the case over to the Justice Department.[9] On Wednesday, November 2, with the backing of the White House, the Justice Department filed suit in U.S. District Court to force University Hospital to release Baby Jane's medical records.[10]

The Justice Department's lawsuit was *not* aimed at forcing University Hospital to operate on Baby Jane Doe, contrary to many reports. It did *not* claim that her civil rights had been violated. In fact, the government conceded that the medical records it *had* seen — those for the first eight days of Jane Doe's life, from October 11 to October 19 — did not indicate a federal civil rights violation.[11]

The question raised by the suit was whether the infant's civil rights might have been violated *after* October 19. To answer that question, the government had to examine the medical records for that period. In forty-eight other instances in which a case of discriminatory nontreatment had been reported to OCR in the previous six months, hospitals had cooperated.[12] Now, University Hospital was balking. The Justice Department sued to force University Hospital to do what forty-eight other hospitals already had done voluntarily: release medical records to federal investigators.

The issues were familiar ones: the privacy rights of the parents and physicians versus the independent civil rights of the newborn.

"The federal government," charged hospital attorney Richard Rifkin, "is claiming the power to meddle in private medical decisions made by physicians."[13]

"Our view," countered U.S. Assistant Attorney General for Civil Rights William Bradford Reynolds, "is that in order to enforce the civil rights laws across the board, it's important that the federal government not be stonewalled or thwarted at the outset. That's what this case is all about."[14]

"Intervention by federal authorities," Reynolds also observed, "may represent the child's only realistic chance of survival."[15]

To Dr. Koop, the significance of the case went far beyond sterile legal arguments over conflicting rights. "We're not just fighting for this baby," he told a television interviewer, "We're fighting for the principle of this country that every life is individually and uniquely sacred. . . . If we do not 'intrude' into the life of a child such as this, whose civil rights may be abrogated? The next person may be you."[16]

By now the case of Baby Jane Doe had become a major media story. The press coverage was one-sided, persistently inaccurate, and marked by vicious attacks on the government for attempting to champion the rights of Baby Jane Doe.

The inaccuracies deserve some attention. Newspapers routinely reported that even if Baby Jane had surgery she would be severely retarded, bedridden for life, in almost constant pain, and unable to talk or respond to any emotion. These statements are almost certainly incorrect.

Most notably, the media repeated again and again that even with surgery Jane Doe would be able to live at most twenty years. The origin of this claim is intriguing.

In the original state court proceedings, Dr. Newman, on whose advice Jane Doe's parents decided not to operate, was asked to speculate about the baby's potential life expectancy.

"How long might the child live after surgery?" he was asked.

"There really is no way of placing a limit on it if surgery is performed," he answered.

"Could it conceivably be twenty years?" asked the cross examiner, apparently fishing for some concrete response.

"Yes," Dr. Newman answered, "twenty years is possible."[17]

Despite the fact that no physician familiar with Jane Doe has ever said that twenty years was the outside limit of her life expectancy, Dr. Newman's vague, almost off-hand, response has been universally reported as the established medical prognosis.

The press also unrelentingly portrayed the story as a conflict between a cold, insensitive bureaucracy and victimized parents. The Los Angeles *Times* branded the government's involvement as "A Sordid Intrusion."[18] The New York *Times*, drawing on imagery from George Orwell's *1984*, decried the "cruelty" of "Baby Jane's Big Brothers."[19] The *Wall Street Journal* also picked up the "Big Brother" theme, savaging what it called "the Reagan administration's medico-legal busy-bodies" who, it suggested, were intent on turning what was "already a nightmare" into "a psychedelic bad trip."[20]

"The premise of these headlines," noted syndicated column-ist Patrick Buchanan, "is that those who want to operate to save the little girl's life are being cruel and dictatorial to the family, while those who wish to let her die quickly are her caring and loving friends. One wonders how Baby Jane would vote."[21]

Columnist George F. Will also marvelled at the New York *Times* changeable civil rights sensibilities. "If a parent and an employer decided to employ the parents' healthy child at less than the minimum wage, the *Times* would demand a federal posse," Will wrote. "But when the government considers intervening to prevent parents and doctors from causing death by withholding treatment, the *Times* champions parental sovereignty."[22]

Indeed, the media were effusive in their defense of the parents' right to be the sole arbiters of Jane Doe's fate. CBS devoted a segment of its highly-rated "60 Minutes" program to this theme, skillfully blending heart-tugging sympathy for Dan and Linda with contempt for attorney Lawrence Wash-burn.

At one point the reporter asked Dan and Linda about an optimistic prognosis for their daughter from a doctor con-sulted by Washburn.

"Those statements are just part of the total ignorance he shows in this case," Dan responded. "He has no right to say such a thing, because the medical records will show quite the contrary."[23]

Of course, the government went to court precisely to find out what these medical records show.

The Baby Jane Doe case is famous because of the legal maneuverings and the intervention of the federal government. But just as interesting are the events of October 11, 1983—the day Jane Doe was born, the day her parents decided, in probable effect, to let her die. How was the decision made?

The courts seem to have held that the decision of whether to treat a handicapped newborn is a purely private one, resting solely with the parents.

It may seem harsh to argue that parents should *not* be the sole decision-makers in such cases. A strong tradition in American society—as well as in the Judeo-Christian ethic—supports the primacy of parental responsibility and authority over the care and raising of children. That primacy is firmly embedded in law, which by and large shields parents from outside interference in the way they govern the life of their family.

Even so, that parental authority is not absolute. For example, we have laws against child neglect and abuse, reflecting society's interest in the well-being of its children. Parental authority may be limited even when it is exercised in the name of so fundamental a constitutional right as freedom of religion. Parents who belong to Jehovah's Witnesses sometimes refuse permission for their children to receive blood transfusions, citing the teachings of their religion. Society overrules them: doctors routinely seek, and judges routinely grant, court orders in such cases directing that the transfusion be performed over the parents' objections.

Granted, then, that parental authority is not absolute and may be overruled in some cases: is this one of those cases? Does the decision whether to treat a handicapped newborn fall into the category of choices that should not be left solely to parents?

It seems clear that it does, for a number of compelling reasons. For one thing, it is all too clear that parents cannot always be counted upon to act in their children's best interests. If they could, laws against child abuse would be unnecessary.

Even parents who *do* have their child's best interests at heart may not be in the best position to make a sound decision about the child's medical treatment. Such decisions are often made under great stress, and without adequate information.

Surely no one can help but sympathize with the parents of a handicapped newborn. Like Dan and Linda, they have eagerly awaited their baby's arrival. They have planned for it, hoped for it, dreamed for it. They have looked forward to the day when they will come home from the hospital with a warm, cuddly baby.

Suddenly their dreams are shattered. A joyful occasion becomes a nightmare of disappointment, fear, even guilt. Instead of cribs and cradles and bassinets they find themselves plunged into a world of operations, wheelchairs, rehabilitation programs. The shock is sudden, the grief intense, the confusion great. In the midst of this maelstrom of emotion and bewilderment, parents are asked to make decisions about matters on which they are almost totally uninformed, decisions whose consequences they will have to live with for the rest of their lives. By any standard, this is an extremely poor way for even the most well-intentioned parent to make such a decision.

Not surprisingly, parents often turn to their doctor for advice. As we have seen in earlier chapters, it is frequently the doctor's estimation of the child's prospects, and his inclinations concerning the probable value of various courses of action, that determine whether or not the child is to be treated.

Most doctors, of course, are not so blunt as some of those quoted earlier in this book—the doctors who disdain handicapped children as "vegetables" and urge parents to "get rid of them." A physician can also guide the parents' thinking by presenting a prognosis for the child's future development that emphasizes, or even misrepresents, potential problems, leaving the impression that non-treatment is the *medically* indicated course of action.

This pattern appears to have been repeated in the case of Jane Doe. The physicians at the hospital where she was born strongly recommended immediate surgery, and it appeared that the father agreed. After the infant was transferred to Stony Brook, however, Dr. Newman presented a considerably bleaker prognosis which apparently persuaded the parents to refuse the surgery.

What was Dr. Newman's prognosis? According to his testimony at the first court hearings, it was that Jane Doe's head was abnormally small, giving her "virtually a 100 percent chance of being retarded"; that she would likely never "achieve any interpersonal relationships, the very qualities that we consider human," nor "develop any cognitive skills"; and that she would be bedridden.

Dr. Newman's prognosis was, to say no more, arguable. His own superior at Stony Brook, Dr. Albert Butler, testifying at the same hearings, seemed to contradict it at several key points. Dr. Butler found Jane's head circumference to be within the normal range for babies her size, and said that the degree of brain damage she might have experienced was impossible to know with precision. He also said that the surgical procedures recommended by doctors at the first hospital—and later refused by the parents on Dr. Newman's advice—did indeed constitute ordinary medical care for a child in Jane Doe's condition.[24]

Dr. David McLone, Chief of Pediatric Neurosurgery at Children's Memorial Hospital in Chicago, also disputes Dr. Newman's prognosis. Dr. McLone's clinic specializes in children with spina bifida: he himself has treated more than one thousand children with that condition.

Having examined the medical descriptions of the child in the court transcript, Dr. McLone takes a very different view of Jane's potential both for physical and mental development. "I would predict," he said, "that this child, in our hands, would have a normal intelligence and would be able to walk with some bracing." The type of brain malformation associated with spina bifida, he says, "is perfectly compatible with normal intelligence."[25]

All of this brings us back to the original question. Was the decision not to operate on Baby Jane Doe an appropriate one, given her condition and prognosis?

The answer would seem to be no, though the issues and the evidence are less clear in this case than in others we have considered.

It would be difficult, for example, to classify Dan and Linda A. as cruel or abusive parents. "We looked at all the options, and everything that was presented to us by the doctors, and at all the best advice, and we decided not to have the surgery, because we thought our child would live with no pain and the time she did live would be a happy time without any suffering," Linda told a television reporter. "We made our decision out of love for her, and nobody can tell us that they think she should have surgery, because they just don't love her like we do. We are her parents. We love her."[26]

But were Dan and Linda misled by the advice they received? Again, there is reason to think they may have been.

When we reconstruct the events of those first critical hours—the apparent decision to operate; Dr. Newman's gloomy prognosis, later disputed by other specialists; Dan's sudden decision not to consent to surgery after all—it is hard to avoid this conclusion: that Dan and Linda decided as they did because they were led to believe that their daughter would die within a very short time and thus be spared a life of suffering.

If so, Dr. Newman's advice may have led to the cruelest tragedy of the entire affair. Dr. McLone notes that a sizeable percentage of spina bifida children who are denied surgery will live anyway, with far more serious mental and physical impairments than if the surgery had been performed.[27]

Is this Jane Doe's fate? Without access to the complete medical records, no one can know for certain. We do know, however, that later accounts spoke of Jane Doe's doctors putting a tube directly into one of the cavities of the brain in order to administer antibiotics. According to medical experts, this is normally done to treat a condition called ventriculitis, a serious spinal infection that invariably produces mental retardation.

Thus, perhaps, did one of Dr. Newman's grim predictions for Jane Doe—that she had "virtually a 100 percent chance of being retarded"—threaten to become a self-fulfilling prophecy. Without the medical records, however, it is impossible to know what the future will hold for Baby Jane Doe.[28]

Were the infant's rights violated? The government tried to find out, but its efforts to obtain access to the necessary medical records ran into a stone wall of judicial resistance and a firestorm of media abuse. The federal court decisions turning down the Justice Department threatened to deal a heavy blow to federal anti-infanticide efforts. There will, of course, be more appeals and more rulings, but they will probably have little impact on Jane Doe herself.[29]

Thus the case of Baby Jane Doe leaves us with more questions than answers. But in one of those questions lies the heart of the infanticide problem. If parents and physicians cannot be presumed to act in the child's best interests in all cases, if prosecutors and state protective agencies are unable or unwilling to get involved, and if courts block all intervention by outside parties, including government officials, then the most ominous question of all remains unanswered:

Who is left to speak for the handicapped newborn?

NINE

Death and Due Process in Oklahoma

What this fiendish experiment proves is that sick babies die when they are denied proper medical care.

— Letter of protest sent to
the U.S. Attorney General

CARLTON JOHNSON WAS BORN with spina bifida.[1] His condition at birth was serious, though no more serious than that of many spina bifida children who receive corrective surgery and go on to live full lives despite varying degrees of physical and mental impairment.

But Carlton did not have surgery. His mother says doctors at Oklahoma Children's Memorial Hospital in Oklahoma City told her there was no point in operating on her son, because he was certain to die in a short time in any event.

"They told me [his chances were] not very good. They said six months to a year," Mrs. Sharon Johnson says. "Everything was negative, no positive, no hopes, nothing. He was going to die. That was the bottom line."

The doctors recommended that Carlton be transferred to a federally-funded intermediate nursing facility, or children's shelter, to let nature take its course. Mrs. Johnson accepted their recommendation.

Some seventeen months later a television reporter visited

the shelter and found young Carlton Johnson there, still clinging to life. As depicted in the film report, the "intermediate nursing facility" turned out to be a run-down suburban ranch house with tattered curtains on the windows and mismatched cribs squeezed into the bedrooms.

Carlton's condition had deteriorated badly. His head, slightly oversized at birth because of excess fluid on the brain, was now swollen to almost twice its normal size. The sac of spinal fluid protruding from the opening in his spinal column had been the size of a walnut at birth; now it was as big as a football and in danger of rupturing. If that happened, the shelter's nursing director said, Carlton would be vulnerable to infection which could cause serious mental retardation and death.

Dr. J.A. Sullivan, chief of pediatrics at Children's Hospital, denied on camera that the hospital had a policy of recommending that children be sent to the shelter, and said he had never treated any patients there.

But documents obtained by the reporter indicated otherwise. He produced an official hospital release form on which an attending physician had recommended transfer of children to the shelter. The reporter also had a copy of a medical examination of Carlton Johnson, which had been conducted at the shelter. On it was written, "No further treatment or evaluation recommendations are made at this time. This child is not a candidate for an active rehabilitation program." The record was signed by Dr. Sullivan.

When confronted with the documents, Dr. Sullivan angrily suggested that the reporter had obtained them improperly.[2] But he did not dispute what the documents said.

Two weeks after the reporter's visit, Carlton Johnson was moved back to Children's Hospital and given an operation. The seriousness of his condition left his prospects in grave doubt, despite the long-delayed surgery.

At about the same time, the shelter where Carlton had spent the previous seventeen months was cited for numerous health and safety code violations and shut down. State officials filed a civil suit against the shelter's owners, charging them with racketeering and fraud.

Carlton Johnson was one of many spina bifida children sent without treatment to the children's shelter on the recommendation of doctors at Children's Hospital. But despite his terrible ordeal, Carlton was one of the lucky ones. He lived. Many others, as we shall see, did not.

Sometimes the most shocking manifestations of the infanticide problem do not take place in middle-of-the-night delivery room crises or in deliberately unattended corners of newborn nurseries, nor are they remarked upon only in confidential medical files or in hushed conversations in quiet corridors.

Sometimes they take place in the full light of day, and are openly—even proudly—proclaimed to the whole world.

In the fall of 1983, as the federal government was formulating regulations designed to protect the civil rights of handicapped newborns, the American Academy of Pediatrics urged the government to abandon its investigation and enforcement efforts and to rely instead on what it called "Infant Bioethical Review Committees" in local hospitals. Such committees, the Academy told the government, would offer "a more direct and appropriate means of addressing difficult issues," and would "ensure that discrimination would *not* occur on the basis of handicap."[3]

But at the same time the Academy was telling the government that hospital committees represented the comprehensive solution to infanticide, the Academy's own medical journal was publishing an article whose message was not nearly so reassuring.

In that article, a team of professionals from Oklahoma Children's Memorial Hospital told how they formed a committee to recommend which spina bifida babies should be treated—and which, like Carlton Johnson, should not be. The babies who were not treated died. The authors saw these deaths as proof that their selection approach worked. Others, however, saw them as signs of blatant disregard for human rights and demanded that they be investigated.

The article was published in the October 1983 issue of *Pediatrics.*[4] The authors were four physicians from the University of Oklahoma Health Sciences Center and a social worker from Oklahoma Children's Memorial Hospital. They described in detail how their "selection committee" worked, and what its results had been.

The committee of doctors and other clinicians evaluates each spina bifida newborn and recommends either "vigorous treatment" or what is described as "supportive care."

"Vigorous treatment," by the committee's definition, was an approach that many experts regard as routine medical care for all spina bifida children: immediate surgry to close the opening in the spinal column, implantation of a shunt to drain excess fluid from the skull when necessary, antibiotics to ward off infection.

By contrast, "supportive care" pushes babies toward death. Carlton Johnson and other babies receiving "supportive care" do not receive corrective surgery or shunts. They are transferred to a children's shelter, where they are given food and water but no antibiotics to fight deadly infection or sedatives to relieve pain.

What were the results of the committee's efforts? Of the sixty-nine spina bifida babies evaluated by the committee between 1977 and 1982, thirty-six were recommended for "vigorous treatment," and all but one (who was later killed in a car accident) survived. During the same period, thirty-three babies—almost half the total—were recommmended for the same type of "supportive care" given to Carlton Johnson.

What happened to these thirty-three infants? Eight were later treated anyway, when their parents rejected the committee's recommendation, and six of these children lived. The family of the ninth infant moved from the area and was not covered in the study.

And the rest? "All twenty-four babies who continued to receive only supportive care died," the article says. Average time of death: thirty-seven days.

In other words, more than one third of the spina bifida children who came to Children's Memorial during this five-year period died. This in itself is an appalling statistic. Other clinics specializing in spina bifida report success rates of 85 percent and higher. The rate at Children's Memorial is less than 65 percent.

Nevertheless, the Oklahoma doctors were very pleased with the results.

"They wrote this article with a great deal of pride," notes attorney Michael Lottman, a former Justice Department prosecutor who specializes in disability rights. "They worked out these really neat criteria for deciding who should live and who should die, and they think the results justified it. Everybody they treated stayed alive, everybody they didn't treat died. Isn't that wonderful?"[5]

Indeed, the authors note with an unmistakable tone of satisfaction that "the 'untreated survivor' has not been a significant problem in our experience."

The number of children who died in the Oklahoma study is bad enough. But even more appalling is the reason *why* they died: not because medical treatment failed them, but because the hospital's selection committee recommended that they not be given that treatment in the first place.

Why? How did the committee go about making its assessments? What are the "really neat criteria for deciding who should live and who should die" to which attorney Lottman refers?

According to the article, the committee works with "no specific critera for treatment," but is generally guided by the views of several physicians and bioethicists whose work we have reviewed in previous chapters. Among those whom the Oklahoma physicians cited as particularly influential are:

—Dr. John Lorber of England, whose criteria for treating spina bifida babies result in an atrociously high nonsurvival rate;

—Dr. Raymond Duff and Dr. A.G.M. Campbell, whose 1973 article in the New England Journal of Medicine argued for letting severely handicapped newborns die;

—Fr. Richard McCormick, whose "relational principle" has been widely adopted as a rationalization for infanticide;

—Anthony Shaw, a leading proponent of making treatment decisions based on an individual's presumed "quality of life."

Indeed, Shaw's "Quality of Life Formula" appears to form the backbone of the committee's deliberations.

> In this formula, QL=NE x (H+S), QL is quality of life, NE represents the patient's natural endowment, both physicial and intellectual, H is the contribution from home and family, and S is the contribution from society.

How does the committee make the delicate judgment about "contribution from home and family?" Money appears to be the main consideration.

Dr. Richard Gross, primary author of the *Pediatrics* article, makes no apologies on this point. "There has to be a way to finance this care," he says, "and if you have a family with limited resources . . . you're going to have to make some compromise."[6]

A case study in the article illustrates how important money is to the committee. The authors describe a boy who received corrective surgery when a second medical opinion prompted his parents to reject the committee's recommendation against treatment. After acknowledging the parents' dissatisfaction with the first opinion, the authors note sternly that "the family . . . has been sued by its local hospital for nonpayment of bills." The message seems clear: Babies whose parents might have difficulty paying their doctor bills are less likely to be recommended for "vigorous treatment."

"Contribution from society" also played a large role in the committee's deliberations, as the equation suggests. The authors deliver a brief lecture speculating on the future likelihood of reduced government spending for rehabilitation programs, and on the inability of some school systems to provide adequate education for the disabled and retarded. They pointedly defend using such factors in making treatment recommendations: "There is no discounting the fact that external circumstances are crucially important in the outlook for the newborn with spina bifida."

But surely it is moral bankruptcy to relegate life-and-death decisions to a crass algebraic equation. And surely it is the height of arrogance for a committee of medical personnel to base such decisions on social and political predictions thoroughly outside their area of competence.

This is especially true when, as the authors admit, "the treatment for babies with identical 'selection criteria' could be quite different, depending on the contribution from home and society."

In other words, under the committee's approach, a baby might be recommended for so-called "supportive care" for *social* reasons, not because his *medical* problems are more serious than those of other infants. The child might die because his parents' income, their social status, or even their school district does not measure up to the committee's unspecified standards. Carlton Johnson, whose mother is poor, black, and unmarried, appears to have fit neatly into this category.

Why do the parents of spina bifida children accept the committee's assessments? Surely they would object if they knew on what grounds their children were being recommended for "supportive care?"

No doubt they *would* object. But the parents, it seems, are not aware of all the factors taken into account by the committee. They accept the committee recommendations as authoritative medical judgments.

Denise Wade, whose son Joey was lucky enough to be selected for "vigorous treatment," realized when she read the *Pediatrics* report that she could easily have been misled. "We didn't know anything about spina bifida," she recalls, "and if they had told us that he was so severely damaged that there was no sense in doing anything for him, we probably would have accepted that. That's scary."[7]

It appears that Sharon Johnson was misled in just this way. "Mrs. Johnson was so misinformed, or just never given the facts on Carlton," the nursing director at the children's shelter said. "She thought he was some sort of monster."[8]

Dr. Sullivan tries to distance the committee from responsibility for the infants' fate. "We don't send them anywhere," he insisted when asked about the children's shelter. "We discharge them to their family. We do not attempt in any way to alter the survival or nonsurvival of these children. We counsel the family. They elect what they want to do."[9]

But Veronica Donnelly, another parent whose spina bifida child was treated at Children's Memorial, says that explanation amounts to "just passing the buck." Technically, she says, the parents do make the decision, "but you base your decision on what the doctors tell you."

Mrs. Donnelly was disturbed to find that her child's doctors may have recommended treatment simply because her child ranked high on "quality of life" considerations. "They're there to heal," she insists. "They're not there to make qualitative decisions about where you're going to be in ten years. No committee of doctors can predict how I would adjust. That should not even enter into it. They have the skill to close a spina bifida child's back: use the skill, close the back. They have the skill to put a shunt in: put it in. Let these little children maximize their potential."[10]

As shocking as the Oklahoma committee's actions are, they are not without precedent. The idea of using committees to handle medical-ethical concerns has arisen before. The track record of such committees is not encouraging.

As early as 1962, a committee of community representatives in Seattle decided which kidney patients would be chosen for dialysis, a new treatment at that time and not available to all. At first, the Seattle committee included what it called "social worth" among its selection criteria. The patient's marital status, net worth, occupation, and "past performance and future potential" were taken into account. The committee later abandoned these criteria—evidence, one report noted, of its members' "profound disquiet at having to 'play God.'"[11] But the idea of selecting patients for medical care based on their "social worth" reappeared in Oklahoma.

Hospital committees also came to play a prominent—and ignominious—role in abortion. In the late 1960s and early 1970s, before abortion-on-demand was legalized, state laws typically stipulated that only "therapeutic" abortions—those that were medically or psychologically necessary—could be allowed. Some hospitals established "therapeutic abortion committees" to review requests for abortions and to ensure that they were truly necessary.

These committees become tools to increase, rather than limit, illegal abortions. Dr. Bernard Nathanson, now a staunch pro-life advocate but then a leading abortion practitioner, describes in his book, *Aborting America,* how he and his colleagues set about subverting the committee process:

> The attack had to be made in the weakest area, the psychiatric indication, which was inexact, unmeasurable, yet sufficiently threatening. . . . The supposed threat of suicide was the logical battering ram. It was just a question of finding a squad of complaisant psychiatrists. . . . .
>
> At first the psychiatrists' letters were detailed and patently serious. . . . As the year went on . . . the letters became shorter and shorter. Every patient suffered from a "reactive depression" and all were imminently "suicidal...."
>
> Like the letter, the committee meetings subtly deterio-

rated. . . . The committees were approving virtually all applications, rejecting only those in which the paper work was inadequate or incorrect, or in which the obstetrician failed to show up altogether. . . .

The members struggled bravely until the liberal abortion law passed the legislature and then quietly yielded up the ghost.[12]

The committees Dr. Nathanson saw in New York were not the last ones to use "inexact" and "unmeasurable" criteria in deciding who should live and who should die. The Oklahoma committee used them too.

The concept of hospital "ethics committees" returned to prominence in the 1976 case of Karen Ann Quinlan, whose parents sought legal permission to remove their comatose teenage daughter from her respirator and from other allegedly "extraordinary" life-support systems.

In his highly publicized decision granting the parents' wishes, New Jersey State Supreme Court Justice Richard Hughes made a point of encouraging the use of such committees in future cases like Karen's. To Judge Hughes, the "most appealing factor" of the committee concept was that it "diffuses responsibility for making these judgments. Many physicians, in many circumstances, would welcome this sharing of responsibility."[13]

In practice, of course, "shared responsibility" often means "no responsibility"; we have seen how the doctors in Oklahoma try to disown responsibility for sending "supportive care" patients to the children's shelter.

In the spring of 1983, as concern over infanticide was mounting in the wake of the Infant Doe case in Indiana, a presidential commission once again recommended establishment of hospital ethics committees to handle a wide range of bioethical questions. The American Academy of Pediatrics followed the commission's lead in proposing its Infant Bioethical Review Committees that fall.

This recurring fascination with ethics committees seems to reflect our society's chronic preoccupation with process over substance. Americans sometimes seem to care less about *what* gets decided than about *how* it gets decided. The words due process become a magical incantation: any decision reached by "due process" is thereby considered a good decision, even if it leads to abhorrent results.

This seems to have been the case in Oklahoma. The *Pediatrics* authors describe in great detail the mechanics of their committee procedure: who sits on the committee, when it meets, how it votes, how the leader is designated, and so on. To them, the fact that a large number of untreated babies die is not a problem, but an indication that the selection process works. "We described a process that I think is a good one," Dr. Gross says. "Virtually all of the babies that were treated survived, and virtually all of the ones who had no treatment died."[14]

The case of the Oklahoma death committee seemed likely to become the next *cause celebre* in the saga of infanticide. In early 1984 a coalition of disability rights advocates, outraged by what they had read in the *Pediatrics* article, sent a scathing letter of protest to the Attorney General and the Secretary of Health and Human Services.[15] "We implore you," the letter said, "to stop the orgy of pain and death that is now going on in Oklahoma."

The writers drew a disturbing historical parallel:

The approach taken by the Health Sciences Center— deliberately allowing a treatable physical ailment to run its fatal course—is reminiscent of the infamous Tuskegee syphilis study of 50 years ago, in which the same method was used to evaluate the effects of disease in ignorant and impoverished black patients. But it is even worse than that; it is an attempt by medical professionals intoxicated by their own power to purify the race by eliminating those who cannot make it on their own.

The letter reviewed the committee's selection criteria and its results. "What this fiendish experiment proves," it said, "is not that predictions of 'quality of life' or even its duration can be made with any certainty, but that sick babies die when they are denied proper medical care."

The writers urged the government to conduct a full-scale investigation of what had happened in Oklahoma. "The facts, just as written by the doctors themselves in the article, clearly demonstrate violations of both state and federal law," charged attorney Martin Gerry, one of the signers of the protest letter and a former director of HHS's Office for Civil Rights. "I think they clearly are violations of state child abuse laws, and of state criminal laws. I think what you have here is a consipiracy to commit murder."[16]

Michael Lottman agrees, and urges that legal action be taken against the hospital. "When you've killed 24 or more babies, you shouldn't be allowed just to say, 'I'm sorry, I won't do it any more.' It's a little more serious than that. You do have a conspiracy here to violate those babies' rights. You do have a conspiracy to commit murder. It ought to be prosecuted."[17]

Whether or not the government investigates, and whether or not the case is prosecuted, the Oklahoma affair stands as stark evidence that the problem of infanticide, and the issues it raises, are still very much with us.

"We share a belief that a human being, once born alive, has all the rights of personhood regardless of race, national origin, sex, or physical or mental handicap," the disability rights spokesmen said in their letter of complaint. "We certainly do not believe that such infants, whatever their handicaps, can be summarily put to death because of a few clinicians' concerns about 'quality of life' or the state of the economy. We fear for the soul of a society in which any group of persons, however afflicted, can be openly and methodically exterminated."

It is to the "quality of life" concept, and its impact on the soul of our society, that we turn our attention next.

TEN

Of Dominoes and Slippery Slopes

"Whatever proportion these crimes finally assumed, it became evident to all who investigated them that they had started from small beginnings. . . ."
—Dr. Leo Alexander, medical consultant to the Nuremburg war-crimes trials.

FOR YEARS, ANTI-ABORTION SPOKESMEN warned it would come to this.

Abortion, they said, was only the first step. Once you accepted the idea that a human life could be ended for the sake of convenience or to avoid a "substandard quality of life," there would be no logical reason to stop with the unborn. The same arguments would apply to handicapped newborns, the mentally retarded, the elderly infirm, and any others who came to be thought of as burdens. If you could kill someone five days before he was born, why not five days after? Why not five *years* after? Fifteen years? Fifty?

Abortion, they said, was the first domino, the first step down the slippery slope, the entering edge of the wedge. Next would come infanticide, and after that euthanasia. Abortion, infanticide, and euthanasia are of a piece, they said. You cannot allow one without thereby opening the way for the others.

No, pro-abortion forces always replied. Don't get hysterical. It won't happen. It won't go that far. We can draw the line.

Is it really any surprise that barely ten years after the Supreme Court legalized abortion-on-demand, infanticide has become a grisly fact of life (and death) in the United States?

"Slippery slope" arguments are tricky. They can be, and have been, abused. The mere fact that two things are somehow related does not mean that one was *caused* by the other. Sunrise and cockcrow are obviously related, but the rooster does not make the sun come up.

And yet . . . sometimes one thing *does* lead to another. Sometimes there *is* a domino effect. Sometimes the camel's nose *does* get under the tent. Wedge arguments are not always the bogeymen that some critics make them out to be.

The ethicist Paul Ramsey explains how to understand wedge arguments:

> The wedge argument does not mean . . . a mere prediction that if we do X we will cause ourselves to do Y, and since Y is wrong we should not start the sequence by doing X. The prediction is based on the *internal reasons* justifying one kind of action and then equally another kind of action. . . . The argument does not say that, because of some sort of physical or social necessity, we *cannot* stop at one or more points down the slippery slope. It says, rather, that where there are no overriding counterreasons for not doing Y for the same reasons we invoked to justify X, there are no sufficient good reasons for stopping.[1]

The argument, in other words, is not that abortion somehow *causes* infanticide. Rather, it is that the rationale we have adopted to justify abortion will work just as well to justify infanticide and euthanasia. Having accepted abortion and the thinking that goes with it, we leave ourselves with no reason *in logic* not to accept infanticide and euthanasia for the same reasons.

And the process does not end here. "All who observe the work of courts," wrote Supreme Court Justice Robert H. Jackson in 1944, "are familiar with what Judge Cardozo described as 'the tendency of a principle to expand itself to the limit of its logic.' "[2] Ideas seem to have a life of their own. They are restless; they seek to grow and conquer new territory.

In just this way, the abortion logic has begun "to expand itself to the limit of its logic." It does not merely open the door to infanticide, but actively moves to enter, and to take us in with it. Ramsey first discovered this when he tried, in the months immediately following the *Roe* v. *Wade* decision, to argue against abortion by showing how it would lead to infanticide. To his dismay, the argument backfired: many people concluded that if abortion led to infanticide, then infanticide must be all right. "The more firmly the connection is established," he later lamented, "the more people who endorse elective abortion may be impelled to accept the practice of infanticide."[3]

This, indeed, is what has happened. For example, one of the keystones of *Roe* v. *Wade* was that the unborn child was not a legal "person" under the meaning of the Fourteenth Amendment to the Constitution. Hence, the unborn child had no rights that could be advanced against the mother's desire for an abortion. It was not long until this "non-person" argument began to be made in terms of handicapped newborns.

In May of 1973—four months after *Roe* v. *Wade* —the Nobel Prize-winning scientist Dr. James Watson said that, "If a child was not declared alive until three days after birth, then all parents could be allowed the choice that only a few are given under the present system [that is, to have their defective offspring killed]. The doctor could allow the child to die if the parents so chose and save a lot of misery and suffering."[4]

In January, 1978, another Nobel Prize-winning scientist, Dr. Francis Crick, argued that "no newborn infant should be declared human until it has passed certain tests regarding its genetic endowment . . . if it fails these tests it forfeits the right to live."[5]

Indeed, the very way people talk about infanticide reveals its link to the Court's "non-person" abortion rationale.

"People love to hide behind the euphemisms that make troubling realities palatable," Dr. Koop has observed. "People who get an abortion can hide behind the Supreme Court and say, 'The Supreme Court says this isn't a person. So I'm not doing anything wrong. I'm just getting rid of a fetus, legally not a person.'

"Now some people are applying that same terminology to newborn infants. Of course, no one has decreed that newborns are not "persons," so these people now refer to the newborn baby as a *fetus ex utero* — that is, a 'fetus outside the womb.' You see how it's done? They take the Supreme Court's terminology of non-personhood and apply it to the baby: "It's really only a fetus, therefore . . ."[6]

Another example of the abortion rationale "expanding itself" has to do with the Supreme Court's decision in *Roe* v. *Wade* that the "right of privacy . . . is broad enough to encompass a woman's decision whether or not to terminate her pregnancy." The Court did not trouble itself to resolve the pesky question of precisely where in the Constitution this right could be found. Nor did it attempt to demonstrate by logic that the right of privacy included the right to abortion on demand; it simply *asserted* that it did, in what one dissenting justice rightly called "an exercise of raw judicial power."

Not surprisingly, this misty and malleable right of privacy has reappeared in other settings. The judge in the Karen Ann Quinlan case found it a handy justification for allowing the parents to "pull the plug" on their comatose daughter. If the right of privacy was "broad enough" to cover abortion, the judge said, then "presumably" it was also "broad enough" to "encompass a patient's decision to decline medical treatment under certain circumstances." But what about the awkward fact that the patient in this case was not able to exercise her newly-created right? No problem, the judge said: "Karen's right of privacy may be asserted *on her behalf* by her guardian . . . and family."[7]

Surely this is a mischievous notion. Karen has a right to be allowed to die, the judge says—but someone else may exercise it for her under certain circumstances. If, like other principles, this one "expands itself to the limit of its logic," the results could be ominous indeed. How many handicapped newborns, or mentally retarded adults, or seriously ill elderly people, might someday be "allowed to die" because someone decides to exercise their right of privacy "on their behalf?"

But the law concerning life and death has taken even more bizarre twists and turns in the years since *Roe* v. *Wade*. The legalization of abortion, coupled with medical science's ever-increasing ability to diagnose birth defects in the womb, has given rise to new fields of law called "wrongful birth" and "wrongful life."

In a wrongful birth suit, parents sue their doctor for failing to inform them that their baby was likely to be born with physical or mental impairments. Had they known, the parents must argue, they would have gotten an abortion. They must show that the doctor either failed to test for potential birth defects or, if he did test, failed to interpret or communicate the results properly. If they show this, the doctor becomes legally liable for the financial support of the handicapped child.

Wrongful life suits are similar to wrongful birth, except that it is the handicapped individual himself who sues, claiming that his handicaps should have been diagnosed *in utero* so that he could have been aborted. In other words, in a wrongful life suit, an individual sues his doctor, or even his parents, *because they failed to have him killed.*

Wrongful birth is already well-established in American law. At least nine states recognize it as legitimate grounds for a lawsuit, and sizable monetary awards have been granted in some cases. Wrongful life has been slower to catch on—some judges have rejected it on the theory that it is impossible to put a price tag on human life—but some observers consider its eventual acceptance inevitable.

It is not hard to envision what the outcome of increasing lawsuits for wrongful birth and wrongful life might be.

In the short run, it will increase the number of abortions. To avoid being sued, doctors may find it in their interest to vigorously recommend comprehensive prenatal testing for potential birth defects, and to clearly offer the abortion option in those cases where such defects may be present. Parents who decline to participate in this kind of "search and destroy mission" may be required to sign a statement waiving their right to sue for wrongful birth if their baby is born with a handicap. (How parents might shield themselves from subsequent wrongful life suits by their children is not clear.)

In the long run, wrongful birth and wrongful life will also add to pressures for infanticide. Our society already tends to see infanticide as a sort of "delayed abortion"; how likely is it to intervene if parents and doctors choose to kill defective newborns who somehow slip through the prenatal screening process?

Moreover, the specter of a malpractice suit may well influence the medical advice a doctor gives to the parents of a newborn with physical or mental impairments. Indeed, some legal observers predict that the law of wrongful birth and wrongful life could well evolve in such a way as to hold physicians who *do* aggressively treat a handicapped newborn liable for malpractice if the child or his parents later decide that his life has become a burden.[9]

The concept of a wrongful life lawsuit—of an individual actually suing his parents for not killing him—is so bizarre as to seem mindless. But it is *not* mindless, and that is the crucial point. It is merely the present legal expression of "the tendency for a principle to expand itself to the limit of its logic." Bizarre it may be, and perverse it may be, but it is utterly logical.

The principle that has expanded itself to bring about the concept of wrongful life is the same one that leads to the "non-person" designation, the same one that erases an unborn child's right to live, the same one that leads to the expansive "right of privacy" that allows parents to put their children to death.

It is the principle that assesses the value of a human life based on its "potential for meaningful existence," or its "social worth," or its economic productivity. It is the quality of life ethic, which has largely supplanted the traditional sanctity of life ethic in modern medicine, law, and society generally.

We have already seen this ethic illustrated many times in this book. It forms the basis of Dr. Duff's decisions to withhold treatment from children he considers "vegetables," of the test of humanhood devised by Joseph Fletcher, of Fr. McCormick's relational principle, of the Oklahoma clinic's approach to selecting spina bifida children for "supportive care."

Where else might the quality of life ethic lead?

We do not need to speculate in order to answer this question. We merely need to read the history books. We have already seen, in our own Western culture and in our own century, where the quality of life ethic can lead.

Dr. Leo Alexander was a medical consultant to the Nuremburg war crimes trials after World War II. In 1949 he published an article in the *New England Journal of Medicine* entitled "Medical Science Under Dictatorship." The article traces the erosion of ethics in the German medical establishment that eventually opened the door to the madness of the Holocaust. One paragraph in particular has proven chillingly prophetic:

Whatever proportion these crimes finally assumed, it became evident to all who investigated them that they had started from small beginnings. The beginnings at first were merely a subtle shift in emphasis in the basic attitude of the physicians. It started with the acceptance of the attitude, basic in the euthanasia movement, that there is such a thing as a life not worthy to be lived. This attitude in its early stages concerned itself merely with the severly and chronically sick. Gradually the sphere of those to be included in this category was enlarged to encompass the socially unproductive, the ideologically unwanted and finally all non-Germans. But it is important to realize that the infinitely small wedged-in lever from which this entire trend of mind received its impetus was the attitude toward the nonrehabilitable sick.[10]

For years, opponents of government-endorsed abortion-on-demand in the United States have been drawing the Nazi parallel.

Abortion, they say, is the new Holocaust: the country dotted with abortion clinics like so many Dachaus and Auschwitzes and Buchenwalds, the evidence of the crime as plain as the smoke that used to rise from the terrible ovens of the Nazi camps and drift across the German countryside, ignored by a complacent populace that knew what was happening but could not face up to it.

Pro-abortion forces do not like being compared to the Nazis. Understandably so: it is not a pleasant comparison, and not intended to be soothing. Even some prolife advocates have been uneasy with it. The analogy is imprecise, they say, and overly sensational. It causes division. It gets in the way of reasoned discussion and debate.

But the shoe fits rather too well to discard. Moreover, the Nazi analogy is even more directly applicable to infanticide than to abortion. However unpleasant it may be to recount, we dare not ignore so forceful a lesson. The German experience can tell us more than we may wish to know about where infanticide comes from, and where it may lead us.

The "small beginnings" to which Dr. Alexander refers, the "subtle shift in emphasis in the basic attitude of the physicians," began some years before the Nazis came to power.

A highly influential book published in Germany in 1920, *The Release of the Destruction of Life Devoid of Meaning*, was among the first carriers of the quality of life infection. The book argued for removing legal penalties for killing what it variously called "worthless people," "absolutely worthless human beings," "those who cannot be rescued and whose death is absolutely necessary," those who are "below the level of beasts" and who have "neither the will to live nor to die," those who "represent a foreign body in human society."

Building on this philosophical base, by the 1930s the Germans had launched a propaganda barrage aimed at the "useless, incurably sick." It was both aimed at and spread by the German medical establishment.

In the beginning, the propaganda was based more on economics than on racial purity. The "worthless people" were to be eliminated, not so much because they contaminated the race but because they simply cost too much:

> A widely used high school mathematics text, *Mathematics in the Service of National Political Education*, included problems stated in distorted terms of the cost of caring for and rehabilitating the chronically sick and crippled. One of the problems asked, for instance, how many new housing units could be built and how many marriage-allowance loans could be given to newly wedded couples for the amount of money it cost the state to care for "the crippled, the criminal, and the insane."[12]

Dr. Alexander says that the Holocaust began here, with the chronically ill, the mentally retarded, the ones Hitler called "useless eaters"—those who consumed more than they produced, who were a burden to society.

Defective children were prominently included in this early target group. By 1939 the German government had established what it called, with characteristic euphemism, the "Realm's Committee for Scientific Approach to Severe Illness Due to Heredity and Constitution." The committee, according to Dr. Alexander, was "devoted exclusively to the killing of children."[13]

The methodology of the killing was familiar. With other victims, the Germans would in time learn to kill by lethal injections or by other techniques. But they killed children by the same technique some people use in modern America: starvation. Frederick Wertham, a psychiatrist who has studied the Nazi experience, tells of a psychology student's visit to one of the German state hospitals in 1939:

> In the children's ward were some twenty-five half-starved children ranging in age from one to five years. The director of the institution . . . explained the routine. We don't do it, he said, with poisons or injections. "Our method is much simpler and more natural." With these words, the fat and smiling doctor lifted an emaciated, whimpering child from his little bed, holding him up like a dead rabbit. He went on to explain that food is not withdrawn all at once, but the rations are gradually decreased. "With this child," he added, "it will take another two or three days."[14]

Are we exaggerating the parallels between infanticide in America and the Nazi era? Consider that according to Dr. Alexander, the Holocaust began with "a subtle shift . . . in the basic attitude of the physicians," an acceptance of the belief "that there is such a thing as a life not worthy to be lived."

In today's America, this same ethic has taken firm root, not only in the minds of doctors, but also in the minds of ethicists, judges, government officials, and ordinary men and women. In a 1920 book, Germans characterized the handicapped and mentally retarded as "below the level of beasts." In a 1983 medical journal article, a noted bioethicist quite openly says the same thing:

> If we compare a severly defective human infant with a nonhuman animal, a dog or a pig, for example, we will often find the nonhuman to have superior capacities, both actual and potential, for rationality, self-consciousness, and anything else that can plausibly be considered morally significant. Only the fact that the defective infant is a member of the species *homo sapiens* leads it to be treated differently from the dog or the pig. Species membership alone, however, is not morally relevant.[15]

In the 1930s, German government officials argued for the killing of "useless eaters" whose lives were an economic burden to the state. In the 1980s, American economists and government agencies are thinking along the same lines.

In 1981, the Office of Technology Assessment, an agency of the United States Congress, published a study of "The Costs and Effectiveness of Neonatal Intensive Care." The report includes a formula developed by Marcia Kramer, an economist at the University of California/San Francisco, that tries to quantify these costs. The authors describe the assumptions that underlie Kramer's analysis:

> The dollar values assigned by Kramer reflected the belief that normal survivors are cheap and economically productive: nonsurvivors are relatively inexpensive; and seriously defective survivors are both expensive and not productive.

The candor of the authors is breathtaking: "seriously defective survivors are both expensive and not productive." They might just as well have said that handicapped babies grow up to be "useless eaters."

The implications of the study are plain: saving the lives of defective newborns costs money—too much money. They will grow up to be "abnormal survivors," and will never be sufficiently productive to justify their continued existence. Society will be better off if they die—or are killed. After all, as the authors put it, "nonsurvivors are relatively inexpensive."

The report goes on to present the formula itself, a complex mathematical equation that makes Anthony Shaw's quality of life formula look like grade school arithmetic. Along with the formula, Kramer provides brief definitions of her terms. One of them explains how a particular symbol is to be modified "if euthanasia is the alternative to care."[16]

And so it has come to this: In the United States of America, in the decade of the 1980s, an agency of the federal government has published an analysis of the cost-effectiveness of euthanasia.

Euthanasia, as we know, came later in the Nazi program. Is it next for us? Having begun where they began, with acceptance of the attitude that "there is such a thing as a life not worthy to be lived," and having proceeded as they proceeded, with the purposeful starvation of defective newborn infants, are we now on the verge of ending as they ended? With abortion-on-demand firmly entrenched and with infanticide gaining ground, can the advent of euthanasia be far behind?

In a sense, of course, it is already here. Infanticide *is* euthanasia—euthanasia in a particular age group. The bridge has already been crossed.

We Americans have not yet experienced the kind of race-purification hysteria that propelled the Germans into the final horror of the Holocaust. Perhaps we never will. It seems likely that the Office of Technology Assessment's cost-benefit analysis of infanticide is the true harbinger of things to come. It may be economics that brings on euthanasia.

That is the direction things seem to be heading. Modern medicine is becoming increasingly bureaucratized, increasingly guided by principles of social and economic utility rather than by humane compassion and divine law. Population trends are equally ominous. Dr. Koop cites government studies that project an "hour-glass-shaped population" by the early twenty-first century. According to projections, there will be a very large number of elderly and a very large number of children, both supported by a relatively small number of working adults.

"Never before has a nation been called upon to handle a situation like this," Dr. Koop observes. "The toddler of today, in the early years of the twenty-first century, is going to be called on to bear a burden nobody has ever had to bear before: to provide for the health and social care of these two large segments of society. It's not hard to envision the scenario. Something is going to have to give, and I'm afraid I know all too well what is likely to give first. There is going to be an unprecedented economic pressure for euthanasia."[17]

Indeed, that pressure is already appearing. Colorado Governor Richard D. Lamm raised some eyebrows in early 1984 with his widely quoted remark that seriously ill elderly people have "a duty to die and get out of the way." Paying for their health care, Lamm said, was too burdensome for society.

Lamm's outlandish statement was applauded by at least one nationally syndicated columnist, who said the governor deserved "credit and respect" for "boldly raising what is certain to become one of the nation's most important issues."

Former Secretary of Health, Education, and Welfare Joseph A. Califano echoed Lamm's sentiments. "One-third of medicare is spent on people who have less than a year of life left to them," Califano lamented. "That's all that exotic, expensive hospital equipment used to keep people alive for another month, or another twelve months." While noting that society presently serves the health care needs of "a phenomenal proportion of our people," Califano predicted that "we're going to have to take care of them in different ways in the future."[18]

What some of those "different ways" might be was suggested by a group of doctors writing in the *New England*

Journal of Medicine at about the same time Governor Lamm made his controversial remark.[19] They proposed guidelines under which it would be considered acceptable to withhold food and water from the elderly infirm in some circumstances. This, of course, is the same "treatment" sometimes provided to unwanted handicapped newborns. One of the authors lamely insisted that the proposed guidelines were not designed to "hasten" the deaths of these patients, though it is hard to imagine how they could possibly do otherwise.

Can it happen here?

We like to think it cannot. We like to think we can draw the line, control the darker elements of our nature, and stop before it is too late. But little in our own recent history gives us grounds for thinking that we can in fact draw firm moral and ethical boundaries.

"I don't think that human consciousness and psychology as it exists in our society today could tolerate euthanasia," a physician muses. "Yet twenty years ago our society wouldn't have tolerated extensive abortion. Our mores change."[20]

Can it happen here?

"I hope not," says legal scholar Yale Kamisar. "I think not.

"But then," he continues, "neither did I think that tens of thousands of perfectly loyal native-born Americans would be herded into prison camps without proffer of charges and held there for many months, even years, because they were of 'Japanese blood,' and the. . .decision largely sustained by the highest court in the land. The Japanese experience of World War II undoubtedly fell somewhat short of first-class Nazi tactics, but we were getting warm."[21]

Can it happen here?

We dare not forget Judge Cardozo's warning—quoted by Justice Jackson in his dissent against the very Supreme Court decision that endorsed detention camps for Japanese Americans in the 1940s—about "the tendency of a principle to expand itself to the limit of its logic."

Dr. Alexander, who foresaw the rise of the utilitarian ethic in American medicine, and predicted the danger of economic presssure for euthanasia, saw it clearly:

> From the attitude of easing patients with chronic diseases away from the doors of the best . . . treatment facilities available to the actual dispatching of such patients to killing centers is a long but nevertheless logical step.[22]

Will it happen here? *Must* it happen here? Will the pressures of prejudice and greed compel us, in the end, to take that long but logical step of which Dr. Alexander speaks?

No. It *need* not happen here. We *can* arrest the process, even turn it around, if we will. We can still prevent the second domino from falling.

Can it happen here? We dare not run the risk of naively assuming it cannot. We are already on the slippery slope. How far down we slide will depend on our willingness to face the implications of our present thinking and behavior.

Part II

Toward a Solution

ELEVEN

Rights, Regulations, and the Role of Government

"The key is buying time—and then taking advantage of the time." —Reagan Administration Official

I T IS TIME TO WORK toward putting a stop to infanticide.
The slippery slope is sobering: first abortion, now infanticide, euthanasia apparently on its way. It seems so inevitable.

But things can change. The downward slide is not inevitable. It is possible to begin turning back by putting a stop to infanticide once and for all.

Decisions about medical treatment are made for dozens of handicapped newborns every day. The term "infanticide" refers to one of two possible outcomes. We need to work toward the other outcome: a decision to treat the child, and to offer a productive and fulfilling life to the handicapped adult that he or she will someday become.

Indeed, the slippery slope could even be reversed. The same logic that finds it intolerable that handicapped newborns be killed can lead to new respect for the unborn, for the aged, for the disabled and the mentally retarded. By working for protection for newborn infants, we can build a new social consensus that will respect all life.

Producing this kind of societal change will take clear

133

thinking and hard work, and it will take time. But it can be done. The time to begin is now. The place to begin is with effective protection for the lives of handicapped newborns who will continue to be candidates for infanticide until society does change its attitudes.

The story of the federal government's efforts to provide that protection is a lesson in applied civics. It is a story with many sub-plots, intricately interwoven and often confusing. It is a story that brings to center stage some of the main actors in the infanticide drama: congressmen, lawyers, doctors, government officials, judges, powerful interest groups. It is a story of power and the limits of power, of what government can—and cannot—do to protect some of its citizens.

The story begins, not in Washington, but in Bloomington, Indiana, sometime on Wednesday, April 14, 1982—less than thirty-six hours before Infant Doe was to die of starvation in a Bloomington hospital. Representative Henry Hyde, leader of the prolife forces on Capitol Hill, had learned what was happening in Bloomington and wanted to find a way for the federal government to save Infant Doe's life. Hyde picked up the phone and called the Chicago offices of Thomas Marzen, counsel for Americans United for Life Legal Defense Fund.

Marzen and Hyde thought there might be a way for the government to intervene. Section 504 of the Rehabilitation Act, a law passed in 1973, makes it a federal offense for any institution receiving federal funds to discriminate against the handicapped. Bloomington Hospital received substantial federal funds. Infant Doe was a handicapped citizen, and it certainly appeared he was being discriminated against. Marzen and Hyde thought Section 504 was worth a try.

Hyde picked up the phone again. This time he called an influential friend who, he was sure, would be interested: Ronald Reagan. The President was very interested, and he acted swiftly in response to Hyde's call. He wrote a memo to the Secretary of Health and Human Services and to the

Attorney General, directing them to pursue the Infant Doe matter.[1]

"Our Nation's commitment to equal protection of the law will have little meaning," the President's memo said, "if we deny such protection to those who have not been blessed with the same physical or mental gifts we too often take for granted. I support Federal Laws prohibiting discrimination against the handicapped, and remain determined that such laws will be vigorously enforced."

As we have seen, Infant Doe died before the government could intervene. Moreover, the administration was to discover that it was easier to serve notice of its determination to prevent infanticide than it was to implement that resolve.

In March 1983, less than a year after the death of Infant Doe, the Department of Health and Human Services (HHS) issued the first version of what soon came to be known as the Baby Doe regulations.[2] Following the lead of Marzen and Hyde the year before, the regulations were based on Section 504 of the 1973 Rehabilitation Act.

It seemed an obvious approach. The Rehabilitation Act had been patterned after the landmark civil rights laws of the 1960s; indeed, much of the wording was virtually identical. The goal of Section 504 had been to extend to handicapped Americans the same protections given to blacks and other minorities. Similarly, the Baby Doe regulations sought to extend those protections to handicapped newborns. Federal law would not condone starving babies to death simply because they were black. Surely it would not condone starving them to death simply because they were physically or mentally impaired.

In essence, the regulations invited nurses to report suspected cases of infanticide.

Hospitals would be required to post a notice in their newborn nurseries stating that "Discriminatory Failure to Feed and Care for Handicapped Infants in This Facility Is

Prohibited by Federal Law." The notice listed a toll-free phone number that could be called by anyone suspecting a violation. The call would alert investigators at HHS's Office for Civil Rights in Washington.

Response to the regulations was swift and strong.

A coalition of medical groups, led by the American Academy of Pediatrics, filed a lawsuit in federal court aimed at overturning them. The regulations were an insult to the medical profession, the AAP said. The warning notices were inflammatory and would only serve to alarm parents and visitors who came into the nursery. The twenty-four hour phone line would invite irresponsible, anonymous complaints designed only to harass doctors and hospitals. The rules raised the specter of Washington bureaucrats with bulging brief-cases peering over the shoulders of parents and physicians.

The judge who heard the case, Gerhard Gesell, gave the doctors what they wanted. He overturned the regulations, calling them "arbitrary and capricious." The "hasty and ill-considered 'hotline' informer rule," he said, seemed to operate more on the basis of terrorism than due process.

While officially overturning the regulations only on procedural grounds, Judge Gesell also suggested that Section 504, the law on which the rules were based, might not actually apply to handicapped newborns, and that the regulations might violate the constitutional right of privacy.[3]

Although the toll-free phone line remained in operation, the warning notices were removed from the nation's obstetrics wards and nurseries. The administration went back to the drawing board.

In the meantime, activity stirred on Capitol Hill. Representative John Erlenborn of Illinois, a long-time supporter of prolife legislation, introduced legislation attacking infanticide from a different angle. By amending a bill authorizing federal funds for state child protective service agencies, Erlenborn sought to define discriminatory nontreatment of handicapped newborns as a form of child abuse. His bill would bolster the investigative and enforcement capabilities of the state agencies, who would inherit primary responsibility for protecting the newborns' rights.[4]

Senator Jeremiah Denton of Alabama held highly publicized subcommittee hearings on the Senate version of the bill in the spring of 1983.[5] The hearings made a forceful statement on behalf of handicapped infants, but the atmosphere of controversy over the original Baby Doe regulations seemed to inhibit progress. The Senate bill was drastically watered down before being reported out of committee, and then was put on the shelf. Congressional proponents of anti-infanticide legislation also went back to the drawing board.

Through the summer and fall of 1983, the Department of Health and Human Services struggled to revamp the Baby Doe regulations.[6] The administration's resounding court defeat had dashed any hopes of quick and effective federal intervention.

Dr. Koop, who spearheaded the revision process, realized it would now be necessary to pursue a more deliberate, step-by-step approach. And the first step, it was clear, was to overcome the opposition of the medical establishment.

A major breakthrough in that area came in November when several major medical and disability groups, under the guidance of Dr. Koop and of Madeleine Will, Assistant Secretary of Education for Special Education and Rehabilitative Services, agreed to a statement of "Principles of Treatment of Handicapped Infants." The statement laid down what it called "very strict standards" regarding care of defective newborns, and endorsed the role of government in protecting the infants' civil rights.[7]

What made the statement especially remarkable were two of the signatures at the bottom: those of the presidents of the

American Academy of Pediatrics and the National Association of Children's Hospitals, the two organizations that had successfully sued to block the original regulations. The support of these two groups was not enough to forestall all opposition from the medical establishment, as we shall see. But it *was* enough to pave the way for the next major step.

The final version of the Baby Doe regulations, issued in January 1984,[8] was a major step forward in the government's efforts to protect the lives of handicapped newborns. Although subsequent court challenges left their ultimate form and effectiveness in doubt, these regulations *are* significant. They give us our best indication of the form that government involvement in the infanticide issue will be able to take in the future. By looking at their strengths and weaknesses, we can see what government can—and cannot—do to put a stop to infanticide.

A major aim of the revision had been to remove the specter of heavy-handed government interference in medical decisions, while retaining effective enforcement of infants' civil rights. The new regulations accomplished this by adding some new features that clearly reflected the give-and-take that had taken place among doctors, prolife and disability groups, and the government.

First, the regulations included a model for what were called Infant Care Review Committees, a modified version of an approach proposed by the American Academy of Pediatrics.

Given the history of "ethics committees," it was not surprising that some prolife organizations reacted to this proposal with skepticism. One group cautioned that such committees might amount to "setting the fox to watch over the chicken coop." A spokesman for another organization went so far as to accuse the administration of "caving in to the God complex of the medical establishment."

Such hostility, however, seems ill-founded. The model committees proposed by the regulations were carefully crafted to avoid the pitfalls of past committee approaches.

The name itself reflected an important aspect of the committees' purpose. They were *not* "ethics" committees. They were specifically commissioned to *review infant care*, from a medical and legal standpoint, not to make judgments about an infant's presumed "quality of life."

The composition of the proposed committees would also protect them from abuses. The model committee would include a lawyer, a representative of a disability group or a developmental disability expert, and a lay member of the community (who could, of course, be a prolife spokesman), in addition to relevant medical personnel. One member of the committee would be designated "special advocate" for the newborn to ensure that the infant's interests are represented and his rights defended.

Finally, under the HHS model, the committees would formulate clear and explicit policies about the treatment of various types of neonatal defects. Proceedings of the committee would likewise be open to outside scrutiny.

The new regulations also placed a much stronger emphasis on state child protective service agencies, specifying their enforcement duties under civil rights laws and recommending them as an intermediate line of defense before calling federal investigators into a particular case.

But the most important aspect of the revised regulations was their refusal to back down from federal civil-rights/ investigation and enforcement as the bottom line in the effort to stop infanticide.

The regulations pointedly retained the twenty-four-hour telephone notification system, which had already proven itself effective in alerting authorities to cases of suspected infanticide. During its first six months of operation—even when notices of its existence were not posted in hospitals—it produced forty-nine complaints that HHS's Office for Civil Rights investigated. As we saw in chapter two, in three of those cases, the mere presence of federal investigators appeared to lead directly to proper treatment of handicapped newborns who had previously been destined for nontreatment.

The notification procedure also included a new feature designed to ensure hospital compliance with the regulations' medical guidelines. Hospitals were required to post one of two informational notices. The first one, Notice "A," stated that discriminatory nontreatment of handicapped newborns was against *the hospital's policy.* In order to post this notice, "the hospital must have a policy that nourishment and medically beneficial treatment . . . should not be withheld from handicapped infants solely on the basis of their present or anticipated mental or physical impairments. Furthermore, the hospital must have a procedure for review of treatment deliberations and decisions concerning health care for handicapped infants." The second notice that hospitals could choose, Notice "B," said nothing about the hospital's policy but merely warned that discriminatory nontreatment of defective newborns was against federal law.

It would seem unlikely that many hospitals would opt for the second notice which, when read in the context of the first, implied that the hospital's policy was *not* to treat handicapped newborns properly. Indeed, some knowledgeable officials conceded that the regulations were designed to prompt hospitals to adopt Notice A for public relations purposes, if not for more noble motives. Once they did so, their policies and procedures would become much more open to scrutiny. Moreover, once most hospitals had opted for Notice A, the requirements for posting it could be stiffened in future years.

Taken as a whole, then, the Baby Doe regulations represented the beginning of a sound and workable approach to federal involvement in the infanticide issue. But they are only a beginning. If they are to be maximally effective, additional steps may need to be taken to strengthen them.

For example, will Infant Care Review Committees really

work? They may need stronger federal oversight. The regulations make such committees strictly voluntary, and the model offered in the regulations is purely advisory. There is no guarantee that hospitals will establish committees or, if they do, that they will follow the model proposed by HHS, with its important "special advocate" and policy-review provisions.

In addition, state agencies will require considerable additional resources and training if they are to bear a significant part of the enforcement burden. We have already noted how child protective services are plagued by severe lack of manpower, expertise, and funding. We have also noted their reluctance to get involved in cases of suspected infanticide: the performances of the state child abuse agencies in the Infant Doe and Baby Jane Doe cases were abysmal.

One way to help the states combat infanticide would be to involve not only child abuse agencies but also developmental disability agencies. Under existing federal law, every state is required to have a Developmental Disability Council to administer federal funds, and to maintain a Protection and Advocacy Service to look out for the rights of the disabled. These councils have greater expertise and better legal resources than the child abuse agencies, and also tend to have an easier time obtaining funding.

Further steps may also be necessary to ensure that someone will respond when complaints about suspected infanticide are reported in future years.

The Office for Civil Rights, whose duty it will be to answer the twenty-four-hour phone system and send out investigative teams, has many other areas of responsibility. It would be all too easy for Baby Doe cases to "fall into the cracks" amid the press of other concerns—especially in the not-unlikely context of a future administration with a weak commitment to prolife and disability-rights concerns.

One important step that could be taken in this regard would be to establish a separate unit within the Office for Civil

Rights specifically charged with enforcing the Baby Doe regulations. If such a unit were established, its funding and personnel would be somewhat insulated from future political shifts, and its heightened visibility would make it easier to hold it accountable for its performance.

The new regulations had been in effect less than a month when they were challenged in court once again. The American Medical Association and five other groups filed a lawsuit in federal court, arguing that Section 504 of the Rehabilitation Act of 1973—the law on which the regulations were based—was never meant by Congress to apply to the problems of handicapped newborns.[9] Even some supporters of the Baby Doe regulations had been concerned that they might be vulnerable to such a challenge: the Justice Department's efforts to obtain Baby Jane Doe's medical records had been rebuffed on precisely those grounds.

Thus officials once again faced the same problem that had confronted Henry Hyde when he first learned of the Infant Doe case: securing a legal basis for getting the government involved in the first place. The government lost the first round when a federal judge ruled in favor of the A.M.A. and struck down the regulation.[10] But the Justice Department made plans to appeal the decision, and the administration seemed prepared to take the case all the way to the Supreme Court.

In the meantime, efforts to establish new legislative protections for handicapped newborns intensified on Capitol Hill. There have been unmistakable signs of progress: Congressman Erlenborn's bill, defining discriminatory nontreatment of handicapped newborns as child abuse and delegating enforcement to state agencies, passed the House in early 1984.[11] The Senate version moved ahead slowly but steadily despite vigorous opposition from the A.M.A.

But anti-infanticide forces still faced long and complicated struggles both in the courts and in the Congress, struggles

that seemed certain to test the political will of future adminis-
trations and to enflame the passions of prolife and disability-
rights lobby groups.

Whatever the final outcome of these efforts, they promised
to sustain what may be government's most effective contribution to the battle to stop infanticide: keeping the issue under
the bright glare of public attention. By continuing to take an
active and visible interest in the problems of handicapped
newborns, the government helps prevent infanticide from
thriving as "the secret crime." Indeed, the court battles over
the regulations, the congressional hearings and floor debates
on infanticide and child abuse, the Justice Department's
involvement in the Baby Jane Doe case, the continuing battle
to safeguard the regulations from court challenge—all these
have already had a noticeable impact on the problem of
infanticide.

"If you had told me two years ago that today, doctors and
judges and politicians and average citizens would even know
what was meant by the words, 'Baby Doe,' I'd have said you
were dreaming," Dr. Koop says. "The so-called 'gray area,'
those cases considered subject to a discretionary decision by
the parents and the doctors, has shrunk dramatically. I
seriously doubt that any doctor or hospital would, in today's
climate, make the kind of decision that got made in Bloomington two years ago. There was a time when those decisions were
very, very common."

Unraveling the legal and political tangles surrounding the
Baby Doe regulations will take time. But according to one
official, time may be on the government's side.

"By putting stop-gap enforcement measures in place and
keeping the whole area under public scrutiny," he said, "we
buy time—time for new medical advances in the treatment of
handicapped newborns to be made and become known, time
for attitudes to change, time for hospital policies and review
committees to get in place, time for the state agencies to get up

to speed. The key is buying time—and then taking maximum advantage of the time."

It will take effective civil rights enforcement to conquer infanticide. But it will take other efforts as well. We have seen how government involvement opens the way for other initiatives. Now let us turn to consider what some of those other initiatives must be.

TWELVE

Changing Doctors' Minds

"I have never had a parent come to me in later years and say, 'Why did you try so hard to save the life of my child?' Nor have I ever had a grown child come to me and say 'Why did you try so hard to save my life when I was born?'"

—Dr. C. Everett Koop

S OME VERY DETERMINED PEOPLE, some of them in positions of power, are working hard to stop infanticide. Every one of them agrees that two things must happen to put a stop to the secret crime once and for all. First, there must be a general change in society's prejudices against the handicapped. The judgment that a baby should die because its "quality of life" will be substandard is, in essence, an expression of a prejudice against disabled people that characterizes our society. We will discuss attitudes toward the handicapped in the next chapter.

Second, there must be a change in doctors' attitudes and actions. Although physicians who allow babies to die say they are merely following parents' instructions, the evidence is overwhelming that doctors call the shots in the nursery. A parent will rarely demand death for a disabled child unless a doctor offers the option. Similarly, a parent will find it difficult to resist the views of a doctor who is unenthusiastic about treating a handicapped newborn and describes its future life in gloomy terms. Babies needlessly die primarily because doctors want them to die.

Some doctors are convinced that disabled newborns are unfit to survive. We have heard from them in this book. These are the physicians, possibly a growing number, who think that babies with serious abnormalities are non-persons and who desire their deaths for reasons of social utility. These attitudes are hard to dislodge.

Other doctors are perhaps more ignorant about handicapped people than hostile to them. They sincerely believe that disabled people lead miserable lives and that the arrival of a handicapped baby is an unalloyed catastrophe for all but exceptional families. These attitudes are accessible to facts— that handicapped people often do quite well and that families with handicapped members are often more closely knit than other families.

These attitudes exist in part because of deficiencies in medical education. Paul Marchand, director of the Washington office of the Association for Retarded Citizens, cites studies showing that the average medical student studies disability for only eighteen hours in the course of his education. Surely here is an area where training will yield some gains—overdue gains in a society with an aging and increasingly disabled population.

Finally, many doctors do not know what to *do* for parents of a handicapped newborn. Obviously enough, the parents are not prepared to face such a situation. They did not expect to have a child with problems. Yet all states offer a variety of services for the handicapped, and virtually every community has a network of families with handicapped members who provide each other with mutual support. This is another area where a few facts in the right hands will accomplish much.

It is important to fill in these gaps in medical education. But before discussing how to go about this, it will help to consider the alternative to the "nontreatment option": Just how *should* doctors treat handicapped infants?

A good man to ask is Dr. C. Everett Koop. He was only the sixth surgeon in North America to devote his skills exclusively to newborns. Before becoming Surgeon General, he was one of the foremost pediatric surgeons in the world, holding the dual posts of Surgeon-in-Chief at The Children's Hospital in Philadelphia and professor of pediatric surgery at the University of Pennsylvania School of Medicine. He was editor of *The Journal of Pediatric Surgery*, a prolific author of technical articles, a clinical innovator, and a much-honored leader in his specialty.

One of his innovations was to set up the first neonatal intensive care unit in an American hospital. Some of the infants he operated on are now nearly forty years old. He keeps in touch. "I have never had a parent come to me in later years and say, 'Why did you try so hard to save the life of my child?' Nor have I ever had a grown child come to me and say 'Why did you try so hard to save my life when I was born?' " He probably has more personal experience with the care of infants with life-threatening abnormalities than any other surgeon.

How would this expert's expert approach the treatment of a handicapped baby? Specifically, how would his approach differ from that of Dr. Duff, Dr. Shaw, Dr. Heifetz, and the other physicians who plead for "death as a management option?"

First, Dr. Koop insists that the presumption must always be in favor of life. He believes that virtually all parents have this presumption. They do not automatically look for a way to be rid of the child, and they do not assume that the baby's future life will be an intolerable one. They will assume that the child should be treated.

This means that the doctor's decision is the decisive factor. Dr. Koop has this comment about Duff and Campbell's willingness to pressure distraught parents to choose nontreatment: "Any physician in the emotional circumstances surrounding the birth of a baby with any kind of defect can, by innuendo if not advice, prepare the family to make the decision the physician wants them to make. We do not consider this 'informed consent.'"[1]

Too many doctors make "cure" and "kill" synonymous, he says. An ethical physician can never do that.

Dr. Koop rejects many of the arguments often heard in discussions about handicapped newborns. One is that advanced medical treatment for these infants constitutes "extraordinary care" that can be ethically withheld. Dr. Koop does not find this to be a useful idea in practical terms for a surgeon who specializes in defects incompatible with life. Yesterday's extraordinary treatment is today's routine procedure. Almost all the infants that a pediatric surgeon sees would not survive "were it not for the exercise of the most extraordinary care and the most advanced technology known to modern medical science."

Dr. Koop also rejects the argument that society cannot afford the great expense of treating these babies. The care given to helpless infants is a test of civilization, he replies. At any rate, medical resources are not lacking in the Unites States. "I have never felt that I was in a situation of finite medical resources," he says. "When I was short a bed, I could find one in an equivalent institution. When I was short of respirators, I could rent a spare. Whenever I needed extra hours of surgical, anesthetic, or nursing support, I could always find an individual willing to go the extra mile."[2]

So Dr. Koop treats babies and usually saves their lives. He will not treat if he thinks he cannot save their lives. This is how he thinks about the possibility of not treating a child in distress:

I do withhold treatment from patients under certain circumstances, but if I do, I have to know three things: an extraordinary amount about the disease process in question, an extraordinary amount about my patient, and an extraordinary amount about the relationship of my patient to the disease process in question. If I do not know all of these three, then I must, as an ethical physician, in any decision process come down on the side of life.[3]

Dr. Koop has a firm rule: "I do not prolong the process of dying." He offers a hypothetical example:

Suppose you're a parent and two years ago you brought me your two-year-old son with a neuroblastoma—a form of cancer on which I happen to be an expert. I operated on him, gave him radiation therapy, put him on chemotherapy.

Things went well for eighteen months. But in the last six months he has been failing. I know it, and I'm pretty sure you know it. I would probably say to you and your spouse, slowly and gently and quietly, "I'm sure you have seen that your child is failing. I'm going to make a suggestion that may seem out of keeping with what I usually say and do. I'm going to suggest that we stop the chemotherapy. Let me tell you why.

Your child is failing. We cannot operate any more. We can't give him any more radiation. If we continue the chemotherapy, I think your little boy is going to live, perhaps, three more months. And during that time he's going to have a lot of pain, and he's going to become blind and deaf. If we stop the chemotherapy, instead of three months it may be more like six weeks. He will slip from life quietly, without pain, without blindness, and without deafness.[4]

Dr. Koop hastens to add that this approach leaves no room for withholding food, water, and basic care. "I have had some tragic, heart-breaking cases," he says. "But my view is that just because you know they're going to die you don't starve them. You don't let their eyes get so sticky they can't close them. You don't make them have pangs of hunger on top of all their other suffering. You feed them, you love them, you cover them with a blanket. You treat them like human beings who have been placed in your care."[5]

Dr. Koop is not the only physician who thinks this way.

"We cannot destroy life," Dr. J. Engleburt Dunphy told the Massachusetts Medical Society in 1976. "We cannot regard the hydrocephalic child as a non-person and accept the responsibility for disposing of it like a sick animal."

Dr. R.T.F. Schmidt, then president-elect of the American College of Obstetricians and Gynecologists, fiercely protested the conclusions of the Sonoma Conference, especially the fact that seventeen of twenty experts would permit direct killing of a handicapped, self-sustaining baby. "This position is not only deeply disturbing to our traditional concept of the inherent value of human life, but is potentially shattering to the foundations of Western civilization."

"It seems to me that newborn babies are often given less than justice," said Dr. Robert D. Zachary in a lecture to the British Association of Pediatric Surgeons. "Our patients, no matter how young or small they are, should receive the same consideration and expert help that would be considered normal in an adult."

Dr. George M. Ryan of Boston Hospital for Women also protested the Sonoma viewpoint. "To actively kill an infant that is living," he said, "is to me repugnant. I think this action is so in conflict with the concept of the physician as a 'healer' that such a decision should not be thrust upon the medical profession."

The battle for physicians' minds is in large part a battle over ethics. The ethics of Dr. Koop and medical people who agree with him are a world apart from those of Drs. Duff, Shaw, Owens, and others we have heard from. The difference shows up in the stories they tell. Those who claim to be relieving immense suffering, the advocates of a speedy death in the nursery, use curiously abstract examples to illustrate their reasoning. The victims are "mindless, unable to think" (Dr. Heifetz), "tiny patients who have no history" (Fr. McCormick), morally inferior to a dog or a pig (Dr. Singer). By contrast, Dr. Koop's examples are richly human, poignant, even humorous.

He tells of meeting the mother of spina bifida girl in England. The woman, a physician herself, had signed her daughter out of the hospital shortly after birth when she discovered that the girl was being starved to death. Because she took her daughter out of the hospital, she could obtain no treatment for the crippled three-year-old through the National Health Service.

"I told her," says Dr. Koop, "that if she could get the child to Philadelphia we would eventually send her home walking in calipers, her urine controlled with an ileal bladder—and she might even become the second lady prime minister of Great Britain some day."[6]

Once he asked the mother of a handicapped boy what was the most awful thing that had happened in her life. She replied: "having our son born with all those defects that required twenty-six operations to correct." "And what was the best thing that ever happened to you?" the surgeon asked. "Having our son born with all those defects that required twenty-six operations to correct."[7]

It is here, in his eloquent testimony to the generosity of the human spirit, that Dr. Koop's stance seems most richly informed by the experience of the human dimension of the issue. "What about the rewards and satisfactions that come to those who succeed in rehabilitating other-than-perfect children?" he asks. "Stronger character, compassion, deeper understanding of another's burden, creativity, and deeper family bonds—all these can and do result from the so-called social burden of raising a child with a congenital defect."[8]

Here are some more examples of the contrast in ethics:

DRS. DUFF AND CAMPBELL: "Some [parents who have let their

children die] claim that their profoundly moving experience has provided a deeper meaning in life, and from this they have become more effective people."[9]

DR. KOOP: "Why not let the family find that deep meaning by providing the love and attention necessary to take care of an infant who has been given to them? We suspect that the meaning would be deeper still."[10]

DUFF AND CAMPBELL: "Seemingly pointless, crushing burdens were important considerations" in letting children die.[11]

KOOP: "We are sure the burden would not be nearly as crushing as the guilt many of these parents will eventually feel."[12]

DUFF AND CAMPBELL: "It seems appropriate that the profession be held accountable for presenting fully all management options and their expected consequences."[13]

KOOP: "We wonder how commonly physicians are willing to be held accountable for consequences that may not be apparent in a family until years later."[14]

DR. SHAW: "My ethic holds that all rights are not absolute all the time. As Fletcher points out, '. . . all rights are imperfect and may be set aside if human need requires it.'"[15]

KOOP: "The discussion of life must be brought back to where it belongs—not to emotional, extreme examples, not to selfish questions of rights, not to expedience, and certainly not to economics. The matter should be discussed in terms of right and wrong."[16]

Dr. Koop and other members of the medical profession and the government are working hard to change physicians' attitudes. The "Baby Doe regulations," which required hospitals to accept a measure of federal oversight over neonatal treatment decisions, were accompanied by programs designed to steer medical thinking on a different course.

Another effort will be directed at medical education. Currently, medical schools pay too little attention to preparing future doctors to face the ethical problems they will encounter in practice. The ethical training they do offer tends to be dominated by a utilitarian world view. This bias is clearly reflected in the selection of articles reprinted in ethics texts, for use in medical schools.[17]

In the fall of 1984, a task force under federal government leadership began a three-year project to develop new medical school curricula. The members of the task force include representatives of the American Academy of Pediatrics, representatives from disability groups, and government officials. The committee is under the joint sponsorship of the Surgeon General's office and the Department of Education.

The first phase of medical retraining will begin in 1984 with a conference on the Baby Doe regulations for physicians and hospital administrators. Videotapes of the conference will be available in local hospitals.

Perhaps the most ambitious federal program with the most far-reaching effects consists of a serious effort to put together a national network of data about support services for families with a handicapped child.

These groups exist in almost every community, but it can be very difficult to make contact with them. The typical disability group is a loosely-structured organization, usually founded by a few parents who had to struggle to find services for their own handicapped children. Such groups have low visibility in the community. Most parents who unexpectedly give birth to a handicapped infant have no idea that these groups exist. Such parents would be greatly helped by making prompt contact with some other parents of handicapped children as well as with local social service agencies which can offer extensive services to the handicapped child and to the parents.

Two data retrieval networks providing this kind of information are already functioning. One is operated in Baltimore by the John F. Kennedy Institute. The other covers the state of South Carolina under the joint sponsorship of the state and the University of South Carolina. The Department of Health and Human Services has provided a grant in order to combine the South Carolina and Baltimore systems into one network that will cover nine Southern states. With time, experience— and more money—the network should be extended to the whole country by the end of the decade.

Once the network is in place, any physician with a desktop computer will be able to get a complete list of local organizations and agencies that can help parents cope with the problems that come with having a child with a disability.

An example of an effective local effort to help handicapped babies and their families is the FIND program in San Bernardino, California. FIND is an acronym for Follow-Up Intervention for Normal Development. Every infant born with developmental disabilities in a four-county area is brought to the attention of a FIND counselor. The counselor coordinates the intervention of a large number of public and private agencies to assist the child and its family. The program pays special attention to preventing developmental difficulties in babies who are born with problems.

Richard was one infant helped by the skills of the FIND program. Richard was born in Loma Linda Medical Center and treated for a succession of serious problems, including congential heart failure, kidney damage, and respiratory stress. When his parents took him home after three months in the hospital, his development was lagging far behind normal. The FIND counselor coordinated a program for Richard and his parents that included help in nutrition, occupational and physical therapy, financial assistance from a state agency, and counseling for the parents to help them recover from the harrowing experience of not knowing whether Richard would live or die. By the time Richard reached his first birthday, he had made rapid progress.[18]

Unfortunately, the San Bernardino FIND program is the exception. Handicapped infants born in most places in the United States will not receive such prompt and skillful case management. But the kinds of services the FIND program coordinates in four California counties *do* exist in most communities. A national network would make information about them available to the people who need it when they most need it.

Will these programs work? Will regulation and education change doctors' minds about the value of impaired newborns, and gradually put an end to infanticide?

Progress will be virtually impossible to measure. It is hard enough to know when needless deaths occur in the nursery. How will we know when they *do not* occur?

Yet we should be able to measure changes in the climate of medical opinion—the "atmosphere" of the profession.

One of the most encouraging signs of this change in climate was the decision of the American Academy of Pediatrics (AAP) and the National Association of Children's Hospitals (NACH) to sign the "Principles of Treatment of Disabled Infants," a one-page statement that reflects the views of the major national disability rights groups. Many observers found it remarkable that the two organizations that led the fight against the Baby Doe regulations would later admit that treatment decisions are not simply up to the physicians and parents.

These are among the principles embodied in the statement:

—Discrimination against any individual with a disability, including disabled infants, is morally and legally indefensible.

—A baby's anticipated or actual limited potential is irrelevant to a decision about medical treatment. The child's medical condition is the sole focus of the treatment decision.

—When it is uncertain whether treatment will be beneficial, the infant's disability must not be the basis for a decision to withhold treatment.

—When doubt exists about whether to treat, there should always be a presumption in favor of treatment.

—Those with responsibility for the care of disabled infants, including physicians and their professional organizations, must inform the public about the need, value, and worth of these children.

The AAP and NACH have also endorsed the Baby Doe regulations and both groups are cooperating with the government in medical training programs and in the development of disability assistance information networks.

Dr. Koop sees other encouraging signs. In his travels to hospitals and conversations with physicians, he finds that the "gray area"—where doctors feel free to inject "quality of life" considerations into decision-making—is getting narrower. Many physicians are rejecting starvation as a "treatment," he says; some hospitals are operating on Down's syndrome and spina bifida infants even when senior doctors believe such children should be left to die.

"Everybody realizes they're being watched," he says. "They're being watched by disability groups, by the Academy of Pediatrics, and they're being watched by us."

The government and disability groups had better keep watching, because discouraging signs balance and even seem to outweigh the signs of hope.

The spirit of cooperation among the medical establishment, the government, and disability groups was severely damaged by the American Medical Association's suit to overturn the regulations. In a strongly worded statement accompanying the lawsuit, the AMA appeared to challenge the landmark "Principles of Treatment of Disabled Infants."

"The American Medical Association believes without reservation that medical decisions involving the care of severely handicapped newborns should be the responsibility of parents in consultation with their physicians and other professionals," the AMA said. "Federal regulatory efforts to mandate a course of conduct to the contrary constitute inappropriate interference with the proper exercise of parental authority."

Moreover, the cooperation of the American Academy of Pediatrics turned out to have decided limits. The Academy successfully lobbied against efforts to put into new legislation what the government had done by bureaucratic regulation. This seemed to indicate that the pediatricians' professional organization would rather not have any regulation at all.

Pediatrics, the journal of the same American Academy that signed the principles of treatment, has been notably sympathetic to the "nontreatment" option. Two 1983 articles give particular pause because they were published at a time when the Academy wanted to convince federal officials and judges that regulations were not needed. One, published in June, was the notorious commentary in which Dr. Peter Singer compared disabled infants unfavorably to healthy dogs and pigs. The other, published in October, was the article describing the Oklahoma "selection committee" for spina bifida babies.

Then there is the testimony of pediatricians themselves when they wrote to comment on the revised Baby Doe rules. A total of 141 newborn care specialists wrote comments on the rules. Only 39 favored them, whereas 102—72 percent of the total—were opposed.

"These children have no future and are a terrible burden on their parents and the nation," wrote an Alabama physician. Said a Texas doctor: "The 'very strict standard' the Secretary of Health and Human Services is trying to foist on the medical community is contrary to the usual practices of that community."[19]

Dr. Koop thinks that the anger of these doctors and others, stirred by the abrupt federal intervention into the nursery, is itself a hopeful sign. The rules exposed what was going on and galvanized disability rights groups, prolife people, and others into action. With the glare of publicity shining on infanticide, a segment of organized medicine eventually decided it could not defend starvation of babies and discrimination against handicapped people.

"It was the *affront* to the medical profession," Dr. Koop explains. "They were being told 'your ethics stink. We're putting a sign up right in your hospital that says we don't think you can be trusted and we're not even going to give you a chance to comment on it. It goes into effect tomorrow.' That's what did it. It turned the whole thing right around."

Yet the rules only started a process of change. Ultimately, success will come only if education replaces regulation and if changed attitudes replace coercion. Ethics must change. Physicians must come to see the quality of life ethic as inherently unjust.

And our society must still address the other large problem— the fact that we treat handicapped people of all ages badly.

THIRTEEN

The End of the
Mythical American

"He's a 28-year-old male who is 5' 10" tall, 160 pounds, a WASP in perfect physical and mental health and with a little bit of money. He's the acceptable person. Our society is designed for him."

—Evan J. Kemp, director of
the Disability Rights Center

D R. WALTER OWENS of Bloomington, Indiana, thinks people with Down's syndrome are "mere blobs." Infant Doe's parents believed that no Down's syndrome youngster could have a "minimally acceptable quality of life." These views are shocking but not exceptional. Many Americans think handicapped people are mere blobs. In many ways our society treats them as if they were.

This fact is one of the keys to understanding infanticide. Babies die needlessly in American hospitals because doctors and parents and many other people are prejudiced against disabled people. They fear the mentally retarded, the physically handicapped, the blind, and the deaf. Disabled people are different. They cannot *really* have a meaningful life, it is thought. They are not *really* fully human. Some say it is merciful to let disabled babies die. Some say that such acts conserve scarce public funds. The root of such views is simple prejudice.

Paul Marchand, director of the Washington office of the Association for Retarded Citizens, puts it succinctly: "Society holds the view that something is radically wrong with disabled people. They are to be pitied, ignored, and shoved away. These attitudinal barriers must be cracked. That would solve almost the entire problem of infanticide."

Marchand's view is widely shared among those working to stop infanticide. The best thing that could happen to protect handicapped newborns is to make our society one that respects and values handicapped people. We need to clearly state that discrimination against disabled newborns is wrong and we need to pervent such discrimination effectively. But prevention is not enough. Disabled newborns will grow up to be disabled adults. Disabled people need education, jobs, respect, visibility, assistance, protection—in short, they need a better life.

Let's look at the world of the disabled.

First, some statistics. In the late 1970s, an estimated thirty-six million Americans—or about 16 percent of the U.S. population—were unable to perform normal work or house-work for six months or longer because of physical or mental impairments.[1] Most of these people are permanently disabled.

The number of disabled is increasing. Only one disabled person in six was born with handicaps. The rest became disabled in later life through accident, sickness, or injury. Some authorities think that by the end of the century there will be one disabled or elderly American for every able-bodied citizen.

What kind of life do these people lead?

Only 42 percent of disabled adults are employed. Approximately one-quarter of all Americans looking for work and one-quarter of those who have given up trying to find a job are disabled. Moreover, some 63 percent of those disabled people who *are* working live at or near the poverty level. Under-employment is a serious problem. Disabled people are much more likely than able-bodied citizens to work beneath their educational levels in the secondary labor force—in seasonal employment, part-time work, and at minimum wage levels.

"A society where less than half the people are working is going to have serious economic problems," says Evan Kemp, director of the Disability Rights Center in Washington, D.C. He argues persuasively that America's persistent economic ills are traceable in large part to prejudice against handicapped workers.

Education—the traditional route of opportunity for minorities—is still largely closed to handicapped people. Less than half of the eight million disabled young people between ages three and twenty-one receive an adequate education. At the end of the 1970s it was estimated that about one million disabled youngsters did not go to school at all, even though a federal law guaranteeing a free public education for all handicapped children has been on the books since 1975.[2]

By measures of income, employment, and education, handi-capped Americans look like a minority group that is experiencing a great deal of discrimination. This is also how many disabled persons sound when they are asked to comment about their life. Let's listen to some of them:

A 52-year-old woman from New York: "Well, I can't go out for too long or go too far because if I have to go [to the toilet] I don't want to be embarrassed. So I just sit here in the wheelchair looking almost like a human being."

A woman from Tennessee: "I was asked to give a talk before the Nurses' Association on "How I Have Lived with Multiple Sclerosis." . . . A lesson was brought home to the nurses in that the seminar was held in an upstairs room, no elevators, and I was not able to climb the stairs and give the talk."

A blind man from Washington, D.C.: "The only problem blind people have is sighted people. We can do anything they can. But they won't let us."

A disabled man in Nevada: "People are always asking me how I live. And I know the real question is *why*."[3]

Note that these people are not complaining about their disabilities. Rather, in their view, it is *society* that handicaps them.

National social policy toward the disabled is marked by contradiction and ambivalence. Indeed, the many state and federal programs that affect disabled people do not seem to be shaped by any coherent policy at all.

For example, the traditional response to the problems of the handicapped has been to shut them away in institutions. This is still our policy. We currently spend $210 billion a year on institutional care. Some of this is necessary, but much of it is being spent to incarcerate people who, with some training and help, could be living and working in local communities. Such community-living programs would not necessarily cost more money, but could be financed by redirecting some of the vast sums currently spent on institutional care.

We keep the handicapped out of sight in other ways. The design of our buildings, sidewalks, and transit systems makes many square miles of urban America as inaccessible to a handicapped person as the surface of the moon.

If more disabled people could work, they would gain in self-esteem, and fewer public dollars would be spent on income maintenance. Yet some government policies actually discourage them from working. For example, disabled people on social security and welfare often have to stay out of the work force because they will lose benefits if they make too much money. Federal policy should put more emphasis on job training for the disabled. Only a small fraction of federal funds for the disabled goes to rehabilitation and job training presently.[4]

The title of the Education for All Handicapped Children Act of 1975 would seem to speak for itself. But its promise of an appropriate education for disabled children is unfulfilled.

The lengthy process of implementing this law in the nation's 16,000 school districts began in 1980 and will continue for many years. Under the law, all handicapped children, regardless of the severity of their disability, are to receive an "appropriate education." But parents of disabled children bicker with administrators over the definition of "appropriate." The Act calls for handicapped children to be educated in regular classrooms whenever possible, but such "mainstreaming" is not universally popular. Parents worry about what their "normal" kids will see, harried administrators resist more expensive requirements, and teachers worry about their ability to teach disabled children.

Some of the stiffest opposition to mainstreaming and community living comes from the handicapped lobby—special education teachers, administrators of special schools, and even parents of disabled children. They argue that these children need special attention in special schools and classes, and they are certainly correct in many cases. Yet mainstreaming is the one social change that could profoundly alter attitudes about disabled Americans. The talents of mentally impaired, deaf, blind, and paralyzed citizens will be recognized and their needs met only if they become visible, accepted members of society's "mainstream."

Disabled Americans face great physical obstacles, but the most formidable barrier is attitudinal—the able-bodied majority's feeling that the handicapped minority is best kept out of sight. It is a short step from pity to prejudice, from paternalism to the feeling that those being cared for don't really measure up.

Ironically, prejudice against handicapped people seems to be intensifying at a time when new possibilities are opening up. Even though social attitudes are shot through with fear and bias, disabled people and their advocates are moving ahead on other fronts.

For example, new prosthetic devices and therapies are

making it much easier for a disabled person to function with some degree of ease. Microcomputer technology has brought some amazing breakthroughs within reach, and medicine is paying more attention to rehabilitation. Some seventy-five rehabilitation hospitals have been established around the country and the National Institute of Handicapped Research has a $36 million budget to support research. The American Board of Physical Medicine and Rehabilitation has certified about 2,000 physiatrists—specialists in rehabilitation medicine.

Progress is also being made on removing the barriers that keep handicapped people at home. In hundreds of cities, curbs have been cut to enable people in wheelchairs to use sidewalks, and transit systems and buildings have been made accessible to disabled people.

Some progress is also being made on employment opportunities for the handicapped. Disability rights advocates often find that they get a sympathetic hearing when they argue that it is costing American taxpayers billions to keep disabled people idle and isolated. Kemp says that almost every troublesome domestic issue—a limping Social Security system, an upcoming crisis in Medicare financing, persistent unemployment, even the booming defense budget—is a worse problem because disabled Americans are idle. Kemp estimates that one tax dollar in twelve pays for the support of a handicapped person who might be able to work and pay taxes.

Some programs even successfully employ severely handicapped people who cannot be employed in competitive situations. One such program is the Public Service Work Crews of Greater Los Angeles, sponsored by the Center in Mental Retardation at California State University. These crews consist of six people: a construction worker as chief and five mentally impaired men, many of whom would otherwise be candidates for institutionalization. They do public service work: constructing ramps for wheelchairs, and repairing and painting public and private rehabilitation facilities and homes for the elderly. The facility pays for materials; the crew chief is paid a salary by CETA, and the workers live off their Supplemental Security Income checks and a small supplement.

"These men *know* they have something to contribute to society," says the program's director. "It would be sad if these men were ever seen as nonproductive citizens and are sent home to live off the dole and watch TV all day."[5]

Yet progress for the handicapped has been slow. There is, for example, little evidence that well-publicized "Hire the Handicapped" campaigns have succeeded.

"I have seen no evidence that such campaigns produce marked changes in employer attitudes," says Dr. Frank Bowe, director of the American Coalition of Citizens with Disabilities. The campaigns do help employers recognize that disabled workers have lower absenteeism rates. "But their attitudes do not change. The reason, perhaps, may be that employer resistance to hiring disabled people is as emotional as it is cognitive. Or, to put it more bluntly, they are prejudiced."[6]

Rehabilitation has limitations; prosthetic devices cannot make disabled people whole. And physical barriers have not exactly come tumbling down.

The problem boils down to one of attitudes. It is not socially acceptable to openly express prejudice against a handicapped person, but rejection and avoidance are common.

Consider your own reactions when you encounter someone in a wheelchair in a public place—in the lobby of a building, at a church social hour, in a store. Chances are you glance at the person and quickly look away. If you are in the disabled person's presence for more than a minute or two, you take steps to move away. You are more likely to react this way if the person has a highly visible defect such as missing limbs or a disfigured face.

Robert Kleck, a psychologist at Dartmouth University, has found that able-bodied people's reactions to the handicapped are a curious mixture of public acceptance and private rejection. Most able-bodied people tell him that they feel positively toward disabled people. But the psychologist finds a different reaction when he measures eye movement patterns, heart rate, perspiration, and other tell-tale signs when able-bodied people are in the presence of disabled men and women. Kleck's studies show that the disabled make able-bodied people very uncomfortable. Those who are "normal" are distressed in the presence of those who are different.

The roots of these attitudes go deep in American history. Many European cultures have a tradition that crippled and mentally impaired people are special emissaries from God who deserve special protection. There is no such tradition in American culture. Americans honor beauty, independence, and progress—not disability. American physicians created terms like "feeble-minded," "moron," "idiot," and "imbecile" as clinical descriptions for mentally impaired people. For years it was widely believed that mental retardation was something normal people could "catch," like a cold, if exposed to retarded people. It was not uncommon for disabled men and women to be regarded as sexual perverts, as carriers of "bad blood," as being possessed by evil spirits.

Myths about disabled people contained a large dose of racism. In the first few decades of the twentieth century, concern over "feeble-minded" immigrants swept through America's intellectual and social elites. Henry Goddard, an early researcher in the infant science of intelligence testing, went to Ellis Island to measure the mental abilities of immigrants to the U.S. He managed to find that 80 percent of Hungarians, 79 percent of Italians, 87 percent of Russians, and 90 percent of Poles were feeble-minded. By contrast, Goddard found that the most intelligent immigrants were from England, Holland, Denmark, Scotland, and Germany.[7] In 1924, Congress assigned national origin quotas in a new immigration law based on the reports of Goddard and others.

Immigration from Eastern and Southern Europe was sharply curtailed.

The great fear was that mentally handicapped people would multiply, sap the strength of society, and drag down the race. During the 1920s and 30s, the pseudoscience of eugenics grew in popularity, with much talk of sterilizing the poor, handicapped, and feeble-minded so they would not reproduce their kind.

Oliver Wendell Holmes, the great Supreme Court Justice and legal philosopher, believed in eugenics. In 1927 he wrote a Supreme Court opinion that found Constitutional sanction for a policy of sterilizing mentally impaired people.

Carrie Buck was a retarded woman in a state hospital in Virginia. Her mother had also been retarded. Carrie had given birth to a girl whom the courts mistakenly thought to be retarded as well. The superintendent of the hospital wanted to know if he could sterilize Carrie against her will. Yes, said Holmes in the Court's majority opinion. "Three generations of imbeciles is enough."

We must "prevent our being swamped with incompetence," wrote Holmes. "It is better for all the world, if instead of waiting to execute degenerate offspring for crime, or to let them starve for their imbecility, society can prevent those who are manifestly unfit from continuing their kind."[8]

Views like Holmes' fell into disfavor in the U.S. when the Nazis gave eugenics and sterilization a bad name. But the underlying attitudes toward disabled people have not changed very much.

Disabled people do not need psychologists or historians to tell them about these attitudes. Evan Kemp, for example, developed a rare neuromuscular disease when he was a small boy and now gets around in a wheelchair. "When I graduated from law school in 1963 I was not an acceptable person," he says. "I was at the top of my class and I quickly got thirty-nine job interviews. I got thirty-nine flat refusals. I quickly learned the facts of life for disabled people. It was the most traumatic thing that ever happened to me."

After his crushing rebuff, Kemp found a job with the Internal Revenue Service. He later moved on to the Securities and Exchange Commission where he won awards for his work. Today he heads the Disability Rights Center in Washington, D.C.

"Our hero is someone I call the mythical American," he says. "He's a 28-year-old male who is 5' 10" tall, 160 pounds, a WASP in perfect physical and mental health and with a little bit of money. He's the acceptable person. Our society is designed for him. Our economy is set up for him. Everyone is supposed to be like him. Anyone who isn't like the mythical American is handicapped."

As our society becomes older, more racially and ethnically diverse, and more pluralistic, fewer and fewer Americans fit the mythical stereotype. Something fundamental has to change.

"The disability rights movement is the ultimate civil rights movement," says Kemp. "The black civil rights movement wanted the mythical American to be black. The womens' movement says 'we want skirts on the mythical American.' Our movement says 'we don't want the mythical American at all.' We don't have to design this country for him. We don't need to make everything the same. We need to break down the myths about the mythical American and build a truly integrated society."

The disability rights movement blends liberal and conservative ideas. It sounds like some familiar liberal themes in its attack on social stereotypes and pressure for expanded rights. However, as Kemp defines them, the movement's goals echo some conservative themes as well. The movement, he says, stands for two things—integration of the disabled into society, and giving disabled people control over their own lives. Kemp and his colleagues are not necessarily fans of government programs. The movement abhors paternalism of all kinds—parents who smother their handicapped children with protections from the world, welfare administrators who would keep them out of work, educators who would teach them in special classes, doctors who don't want to treat them at birth or in later life.

An editorial in one of the movement's publications articulated its spirit and applied it to the problem of nontreatment of handicapped newborns:

> If anything is a cornerstone of disability rights, it is that we have control over our own bodies, and we are in charge of making decisions about our own lives. We. Disabled people. Not our parents. Not our doctors. For us, these people have long hindered and held us back. We do not consider such people to speak "for" us.
>
> That is the problem with this situation: newborn babies cannot speak for themselves. Left to their parents' and doctors' speaking for them, asking that they be allowed to die, sounds suspect to us.[9]

"We need a massive educational effort," Kemp says. "We have to show that disabled people can be contributing members of society, can be integrated, can be self-sufficient, that they can be loving, that they can have children, that they're not a burden to society, that they can lead a happy life if they're in a wheelchair, or if they have cerebral palsy, or if they have Down's syndrome.

"Attitudes have to change. That's the only answer. People really don't think the Constitution of the United States protects handicapped children. It won't solve the problem to pass a law to say that it does. A law could even do harm if it makes people think that that solves the problem. The solution is a new attitude. We have to broaden the number and kind of people who are acceptable in this society, who are regarded as real human beings."

How can we change attitudes? Kemp wants to build a coalition of disability, elderly, and prolife groups that could determine the outcome of elections by the end of the 1980s. Groups representing the disabled and elderly already work closely together; there is considerable overlap in these two categories. The disability and prolife groups got together over the Baby Doe regulations. If the same kind of cost-benefit analysis that we see in the intensive care nursery gets applied to nursing homes and geriatric care, older Americans may suddenly find themselves actively and urgently prolife.

Political muscle could help change attitudes. In fact, an effective political organization—one that is respected and feared—is probably a precondition for any thorough attitudinal change about handicapped people.

Education has real potential for changing attitudes. "The waves of history are on our side," says Kemp. "We're starting to tolerate differences among people. Even doctors are thinking differently—the younger ones. Doctors under thirty-five know what the disability rights movement is all about."

To conquer prejudice, disabled people must become more and more visible in our society. A number of forces may well combine to bring this about: mainstreaming in the schools, removal of physical barriers, prosthetic devices that aid mobility, and the increasing political awareness of the disabled themselves. Attitudes will change when people realize that handicapped men and women are people like everyone else.

"People want to know what life is like in a wheelchair," says Kemp. "My answer is that it sure beats the alternative—which is to stay in bed. My wheelchair frees me. In fact, there are two things I need in order to function—my wheelchair and my eyeglasses. I need the glasses much more than I need the wheelchair. Without them I am practically blind.

"It used to be peculiar to wear glasses. No one thinks anything of it now. We need to get to the point where people barely notice that someone is in a wheelchair."

FOURTEEN

Whose Life Is Worth Living?

What is it like to be disabled? It's happy, it's sad, it's exciting, it's frustrating, it's probably just like being non-disabled. Being disabled is not intrinsically a burden.

—Sondra Diamond

D R. RAYMOND DUFF AND DR. A.G.M. CAMPBELL wrote their famous 1973 article in *The New England Journal of Medicine* in part to generate discussion about the practice of letting certain disabled babies die. They succeeded. National news weeklies picked up the story and treated the Yale doctors sympathetically. *Newsweek*'s story was accompanied by a picture of Dr. Duff peering thoughtfully at a baby in an incubator. The magazine quoted him as saying this: "The public has got to decide what to do with vegetated individuals who have no human potential. We doctors can't solve these problems alone."[1]

The story and the quote incensed a psychologist named Sondra Diamond. *Newsweek* published her angry letter to the editor:

I'll wager my entire root system and as much fertilizer as it takes to fill Yale University that you have never received a letter from a vegetable before this one, but, much as I resent

171

the term, I must confess that I fit the description of a "vegetable" as defined in the article "Shall This Child Die?"

Due to severe brain damage incurred at birth, I am unable to dress myself, toilet myself, or write; my secretary is typing this letter. Many thousands of dollars had to be spent on my rehabilitation and education in order for me to reach my present professional status as a Consulting Psychologist. My parents were also told, 35 years ago, that there was "little or no hope of achieving meaningful 'humanhood'" for their daughter. Have I reached "humanhood?" Compared with Doctors Duff and Campbell I believe I have surpassed it!

Instead of changing the law to make it legal to weed out us "vegetables," let us change the laws so that we may receive quality medical care, education, and freedom to live as full and productive lives as our potentials allow.

Whose life is worth living? Who is to make quality-of-life judgments about babies born with handicaps? Who is to deny that Dr. Diamond has been blessed with a fuller measure of humanhood than Dr. Duff?

Earlier we reviewed some grim statistics about the plight of disabled people in the U.S. and listened to some of them describe how difficult it is to find work, to get around, and to win respect. But now let's listen to some of them talk about their disabilities. One of the hardest things for an able-bodied person to grasp is what having a disability is really like.

"What is it like to be disabled?" asks Sondra Diamond. "It's happy, it's sad, it's exciting, it's frustrating, it's probably just like being non-disabled."

"It is too easy to project how you think *you* might feel if you were physically disabled," she says. "Being disabled is not the same as thinking about what it would be like if you were disabled. Being disabled is not intrinsically a burden. It only becomes so when society makes it difficult to function as a normal person."[2]

Consider the case of an extraordinary young man named Craig. Craig has severe disabilities; he was born without a left leg and without arms below the elbows. When he was born, his father told his mother "This one needs our love more." The love paid off.

"I'm very glad to be alive," Craig says. "I live a full, meaningful life. I have many friends and many things I want to do in life. I think the secret of living with a handicap is realizing who you are—that you're a human being, somebody who is very special—looking at the things that you *can* do in spite of your handicap, and maybe even through your handicap."[3]

Craig has done remarkable things: he earned a degree in philosophy from Cal State and was studying for the ministry when he was interviewed. And Craig's surprising comment that a handicap can be a source of strength is not unique to him.

Consider the case of Stephen Hawking, a cosmologist at Cambridge University and one of the best-known disabled people in the world. Hawking is one of the world's leading experts on such topics as black holes, the origin of the universe, and the fate of the cosmos. When he was a graduate student he was stricken with amyotrophic lateral sclerosis (ALS), also known as Lou Gehrig's disease after the famous baseball player who died from it. Hawking is almost completely paralyzed. His speech is virtually unintelligible. He gets around in a motorized wheelchair. His intellect is one of the finest in the world, but he cannot turn the pages of a book.

"I think I am happier now than I was before it (ALS) started," Hawking says. "Before the disease set on, I was very bored with life. I drank a fair amount, I guess; didn't do any work. It was really a rather pointless existence. When one's expectations are reduced to zero, one really appreciates everything that one does have."[4]

Not all disabled people are psychologists like Dr. Diamond, philosophy graduates like Craig, or cosmologists like Dr.

Hawking. Most of them are ordinary people like the rest of us. Their feelings about being handicapped closely resemble the feelings most of us have—or wish we had—about being normal.

One evening Dr. Koop hosted a unique conversation. He invited some of the patients he had operated on in years past to come together to discuss life with their disabilities. They ranged in age from eleven to thirty years old. Four had been born with problems that would have swiftly killed them if Dr. Koop had not operated. Four others had developed lethal problems in early childhood. None of them was "able-bodied." This is a sample of their comments:

Because the start was a little abnormal, it doesn't mean you're going to finish that way. I'm a normal, functioning human being, capable of doing anything anyone else can.

At times it got very hard, but life is certainly worth living. I married a wonderful guy and I'm just so happy.

At the beginning it was a little difficult going back to school after surgery, but then things started looking up, with a little perseverance and support. I am an anesthetist and I'm happily married. Things are going great for me.

I really think that all my operations and all the things I had wrong with me were worth it, because I really enjoy life and I don't really let the things that are wrong with me bother me.

If anything, I think I've had an added quality to my life—an appreciation of life. I look forward to every single morning.

Most of the problems are what my parents went through with the surgery. I've now been teaching high school for eight years and it's a great joy.

They spend millions of dollars to send men to the moon. I think they can spend any amount necessary to save some-one's life. A human life is so important because it's a gift—

not something that you can give, so you really don't have the right to take it either.

I really don't consider myself handicapped. Life is just worth living.[5]

Remarkably enough, these men and women saw themselves simply as ordinary people—teachers, nurses, homemakers, students—living ordinary lives, even though one had twenty-seven operations to correct multiple defects, another has no tongue, another had his colon transplanted to replace an absent esophagus, and another has a face badly disfigured from a tumor.

These men and women are normal people. It would have been tragically wrong to conclude that something terrible and burdensome happened when they were born. Handicapped children have problems, but *they* are not "problems."

This is the message of Carl and Rachel Rossow of Ellington, Connecticut. The Rossows have adopted numerous severely handicapped children since 1971, and have become well known for their work in promoting special needs adoptions. Yet they insist that they have a normal American family. "Sometimes people will make comments to us that we're special," says Rachel Rossow. "And it bothers us, because we're really not."

Rachel Rossow spoke those words before television cameras to a committee of U.S. Senators in Washington in April 1983. She and Carl, accompanied by their three natural and their eleven adopted children, had been invited to Washington to meet the President and give testimony on legislation to protect handicapped newborns. Those present in the hearing room were moved by their testimony. There *is* something special about the Rossows, but their most important message might be that families with handicapped members can be like any family.

"They are children with the same hopes, and dreams, and fears as every other child," says Rachel. Eddy, who lacks fingers and one leg, attends Ellington High School and likes to ski. Simone, confined to a wheelchair, is a cheerleader at Ellington High. Patrick, a good student and avid football fan, was born with spina bifida and nearly died because his doctors recommended withdrawing treatment.

When children are in wheelchairs "you have to do things a little different," says Carl Rossow. "But you have to address the same problems as for every other child."[6]

The Rossows personify a little-noted aspect of the infanticide issue—the availability of adoption. Virtually all disabled infants who are singled out for death could be adopted by couples who are eager to have children. Handicapped people think their lives are worth living; so do many able-bodied men and women who want to add disabled and needy children to their families.

There are many reasons why handicapped newborns are not adopted more frequently than they are. Some parents are convinced that death is the most merciful fate for a handicapped baby. Others cannot stand the idea of giving up their biological offspring; they would prefer that the child die rather than give it up for adoption. Some parents do not even consider adoption. They do not think of it; no one mentions it.

There is, in fact, an enormous pool of children who should be adopted, a pool matched if not exceeded by adults who want to adopt.

The numbers are staggering. There may be as many as 750,000 American children in foster care settings—that is, children who live with families at public expense because their natural parents cannot or will not take care of them.[7] Many of these children are regarded as "special needs children." They are disabled, emotionally disturbed, or mentally impaired. They are beyond the prime "adoptable" age. Some of them are sibling groups who need to be placed together.

The U.S. government says that about 50,000 of these children are legally free for adoption and are simply waiting for parents to come along. Some adoption advocates say the real figure is closer to 100,000 or even higher.[8] At the same time, Dorcas Hardy, a federal official working on adoption policy says flatly that "there is a family somewhere for every waiting child, no matter how complex his or her needs."[9] Why then haven't these children been adopted?

Bureaucratic rules and red tape are among the reasons. The children are usually cared for by state welfare agencies; parents willing to adopt children with special needs typically work through private agencies. The public and private agencies do not talk to each other very much. Many social workers are convinced that the disabled children they are maintaining in foster care *cannot* be adopted and so they do little to help them to join permanent families.

"There are many private, non-profit agencies licensed for child-placing who have waiting lists of approved adoptive families," says Candace Mueller, an official of the National Committee for Adoption. "But they cannot serve these families because the public child welfare sector does not work vigorously enough to see that children growing up in foster care are legally freed for adoption."[10]

Many children in foster care cannot be adopted because their natural parents will not give up their parental rights, even though their children would be better off in a permanent situation. This is a sensitive area. Public policy should facilitate adoption where it is desirable and also pay proper respect to parental rights. Nevertheless, some children stay in foster care too long because parents who cannot raise them will not relinquish their authority.[11]

Some public policies actually *discourage* adoption. Certain federal programs that aid state welfare agencies make it more lucrative for agencies to keep children in foster care than to free them for adoption. Many state child welfare agencies will not certify families for adoption if a private adoption agency requests it. Some states will not give Medicaid benefits to adopted disabled children.[12]

Adoption advocates and public policy-makers are quietly working on many fronts to facilitate adoption. A National Adoption Exchange matches adoptive parents with available children on a nation-wide basis. Other information exchanges recruit adoptive parents and make referrals. Adoptions by minority and low to moderate income families are becoming more frequent. Robert W. DeBolt, founder of Aid to Adoption of Special Kids (AASK), reports that 85 percent of the families that adopt through AASK have incomes less than $20,000 a year, and that 65 percent are rural families.

Adoption should be arranged for handicapped newborns more frequently than it is. "We have a waiting list of parents who are willing to adopt." says Kent Smith, president of the Spina Bifida Association. Says disability rights attorney Michael Lottman, "I have examples of very severely retarded, physically deformed—to me, honestly, somewhat grotesque-appearing children—and they have loving parents who've adopted them."

"The National Committee's member agencies are knowledgeable about the positive possibilities of the adoption of handicapped infants," says Toni McHugh, chairman of the National Committee for Adoption. "We believe that making this option available to parents in distress should be an essential component of any health facility's services to handicapped infants and their parents."

Mrs. McHugh makes the interesting suggestion that parents' rights be terminated automatically if they do not consent to treatment for their disabled infant, and adoption procedures started immediately. At the very least, she says, decision-making should be slowed down so that parents can learn about their baby's handicap, talk to other parents of disabled children, and consider adoption if they wish.[13]

Whose life is worth living? After hearing from disabled people who enjoy their lives and parents who want to bring handicapped children into their families, to ask such a question seems almost grotesque. Those who speak gloomily of "quality of life" know little about the real lives of disabled people and those who love them.

Let us end with a comment from Marilyn Lovelace. Mrs. Lovelace's daughter, Terry, was born with spina bifida. She was treated at Oklahoma Children's Hospital before doctors at that facility designed their notorious selection process which led to the deaths of twenty-four babies. Mrs. Lovelace suspects Terry would have died, too, if the selection process had been in effect when she was born.

"She's given so much," she says of her daughter. "Nothing can take from that. And if I didn't have her, there's no telling where I would be right now, because she means that much to me and to my life, and to my children's lives, and to my husband's life. Without Terry, I don't know what would happen to us."[14]

FIFTEEN

Paying the Price

WE HAVE SEEN many disturbing things in this book.
We have seen doctors abandon their familiar role as compassionate healers to become dealers of death to handicapped infants.

We have seen philosophers, theologians, and other ethicists justify the killing of these children with subtle—and sometimes not-so-subtle—attacks on their presumed "quality of life."

We have seen local prosecutors and state child-abuse agencies turn their backs on helpless children in their hour of greatest need.

We have seen federal judges block the efforts of those trying to protect the civil rights of disabled newborns.

We have seen some of the most ghastly events of human history begin to repeat themselves as American society slides ever further down the slippery slope of abortion, infanticide, and euthanasia.

We have seen a government agency publish an outrageous analysis of the cost-effectiveness of euthanasia, while prominent public officials speak of the elderly's "duty to die and get out of the way."

Most wrenching of all, we have seen the children.

Infant Doe, cruelly starved to death in Bloomington, Indiana.

Baby Jane Doe, denied corrective surgery, apparently doomed to a foreshortened life of tragically unnecessary physical and mental impairment.

Carlton Johnson, set aside to die on the recommendation of a committee who thought he did not deserve to be treated.

These tragic cases are unique only in the notoriety they have attained. For the most part, infanticide is still a *secret* crime. For every baby with Down's syndrome or spina bifida or some other defect whose final agonies find their way onto the front pages of newspapers, how many others slip away quietly, unnoticed by anyone save those who decided on and brought about their deaths?

We can harbor no illusions. We have heard and seen too much—startlingly candid statements from doctors, revealing reports from nurses and other medical personnel, newspaper and television accounts, anonymous complaints to federal authorities. Infanticide is an ugly but undeniable reality of modern American life. Dr. Koop's provocative statement to his fellow pediatricians in 1976 is just as true today: "You all know that infanticide is being practiced right *now* in this country."

How can we put a stop to infanticide once and for all?

To begin with, we must see the problem clearly. In large measure, that has been the aim of this book: to help us understand where infanticide comes from, how and why it happens, where it may lead us. To do otherwise is to delude ourselves, cripple our efforts to reach a solution, and leave ourselves vulnerable to yet greater evils.

We must, of course, be careful not to oversimplify. Treatment decisions for handicapped newborns can present genuine difficulties. Though the presumption must always favor life, we should not be afraid to acknowledge that some cases do fall into a "gray area" where medical opinions may differ and ethical dilemmas become difficult. There are situations in which treatment may legitimately be withheld.

At the same time we must recognize, and make clear to others, that such "hard cases" are rare, and in any event do not lie at the heart of the infanticide debate. Infanticide, as we have described it in this book, occurs when babies who could be saved are instead singled out for death because of prejudice, fear, or economic inconvenience; they die, not because medical science *cannot* save them, but because someone *will not* save them.

We must also be careful not to fill our field of vision so completely with the problem that we become unable to see the way to a solution. Confronting the reality of infanticide can, if we are not careful, paralyze us into despair rather than galvanize us into action.

For we have also seen many hopeful things in this book. Promising beginnings have been made on many fronts. Resources have been mobilized, avenues for involvement have been opened, mechanisms for change have been put in place. Most important of all, the glare of publicity has pushed back the shroud of secrecy under which infanticide has flourished.

This is not to take Pollyanna's view of the situation. There is much still to be done. The entire area seems to be governed by a kind of perverse Murphy's Law: if anything can go wrong for handicapped newborns, it frequently does, and with tragic results.

So we dare not relax. Yet surely the way to a solution lies not in a gloomy fixation on actual and potential problems, but in a hard-headed and large-hearted dedication to making the most of every opportunity. Solutions are within reach, and confident people can reach them.

Capitalizing on the promising beginnings that have been made, however, will require a unified, coordinated strategy. Obviously, infanticide is a multi-faceted problem; an overall strategy for its elimination will need to reflect this complexity. But the broad outlines of such a strategy, as we have attempted to sketch in this book, seem clear: protection of the civil rights of handicapped newborns; a change in the ethics and attitudes of broad segments of the American medical profession; a substantial reorientation of society's attitudes toward the disabled and the mentally retarded. In the long run, none of these three main points can stand without the others. Law enforcement will ultimately fall short unless medical practices are changed; doctors will be unlikely to alter their views of the handicapped until the society around them does so; and so on.

Of course, it is easier to state such a strategy than to implement it. But we must keep the broad plan in view as we pursue the many narrowly focused initiatives that must be undertaken.

And there can be no question that the effort against infanticide will need to be waged on many fronts simultaneously. The "knock-out punch" is a tempting solution, but we dare not pin all our hopes on it.

It will not be enough to wait for the government to impose a final and complete solution by force of law. No such solution can be imposed. Attitudes must be changed. Advances in medical care must be made more widely available. Ethics must be turned around. Legal remedies must be sought out. Government policies must be adopted and implemented. Resources must be generated. One by one, doctors and parents and hospitals and state agencies and legislatures must be reached. One by one, handicapped newborns must be protected and provided for. Infanticide stems from a complex web of attitudes and social factors. It will take time and persistence to unravel them.

This, indeed, is the way of all social change in America. Every successful societal revolution of the past generation has been waged as guerrilla warfare: chipping away at the problem in every available arena, with every available weapon, at every level. Decisive final victories follow upon years of grass-roots activity.

The pro-abortion movement, for example, scored a major triumph with the 1973 Supreme Court decision in *Roe* v.

Wade. In a single dramatic move, the Court brushed aside the abortion laws of all fifty states and dealt a crushing blow to the prolife movement. But the 1973 Court decision represented the culmination of a persistent, determined campaign waged for years in medical societies, newspaper editorials, political campaigns, state legislatures—anywhere, in fact, where there was an inch of territory to be taken. So it was with abortion, so it was with environmental protection before that, so it was with civil rights before that. So it must be with infanticide.

Developing this kind of multi-faceted effort will require that we learn to see the problems of handicapped infants in a broader context.

In examining the problem of infanticide, we have focused most of our attention on what happens in the minutes and hours and days immediately following the birth of a handicapped newborn. This is the time when crucial, and usually irrevocable, decisions are made. The sum total of many years of ethical training, professional competence, resource availability, attitudes toward the handicapped, awareness of legal ramifications, hospital and governmental policies—all are focused, like so many beams of light through a magnifying glass, onto parents and physicians in this one intense moment of choice.

It is not surprising, then, that most efforts at stopping infanticide have also converged on this critical time period. Telephone alert systems, investigations by state and federal agencies, intervention by hospital review committees—all are focused largely on either guiding or policing parents and doctors as they make the initial decisions about how a particular newborn is to be treated.

Seen in this light, infanticide is, clearly and emphatically, a pro-life issue. All energy is directed to a single, compelling purpose: *keep the child alive*. There will be time later to consider questions concerning how to care for and raise the child. But during those first hours and days, the issue is simply one of life or death. Fail at this point, and the other questions will never arise.

Once this first step—saving the child's life—has been taken, longer-range questions come immediately into view. Today's handicapped infant will be tomorrow's handicapped pre-schooler, teenager, adult. How will his family adapt? What kind of schooling will he get? Will he be able to find a job? How will society accept him and provide for his special needs?

Infanticide is more than a prolife matter. In the long run, it is just as much a disability rights matter. The intrinsic worth of each human being compels our concern, not only at birth, but throughout life.

One of the more encouraging aspects of the struggle against infanticide is the way it has brought together prolife and disability-rights activists—often to the mutual consternation of both. Disability-rights activists, who tend to identify themselves with liberal politics, have been somewhat wary of prolifers, who generally stand to the righthand side of the political spectrum. Conversely, prolife activists have had little past experience with disability groups.

But handicapped newborns are neither liberals nor conservatives, Democrats or Republicans. They are extraordinarily vulnerable human beings in need of help. Those who would provide that help must learn to reach across political and ideological lines and make common cause in defense of human life and human dignity.

Another crucial element in implementing a long-range strategy, as we have seen, is buying time by keeping attention focused on the problem.

Until the Infant Doe case and its aftermath, there is reason to believe that some doctors were quietly dispatching handi-capped newborns virtually as a routine procedure. We could see a return to infanticide-as-usual if the issue is allowed to fade away.

There is always a danger that infanticide could one day become accepted by default, that it could become so widespread that society decides there is no reason not to legalize "what is happening anyway." That is why we must keep infanticide under the bright glare of publicity, and refuse to let it flourish as a secret crime.

There are many ways this can be done. Legal, legislative, and bureaucratic efforts by government can have a powerful effect on the public consciousness, so long as government retains the political will to take a stand on behalf of handicapped newborns. Aggressive political action by citizens concerned about infanticide can help sustain and bolster that will.

Next, groups that have yet to become informed and take a stand on this issue can do so. In particular the churches, many of whom have been active in other prolife concerns, have been noticeably missing from the infanticide debate. There is a great need for Christians to speak out forcefully on behalf of the sanctity of life of handicapped newborns and their entitlement to society's care and concern.

Perhaps most of all, prolife and disability-rights groups, who have already become deeply involved in the infanticide struggle, can remain vigilant. They can continue to call attention to the problem in ways that result in fruitful and responsible individual, group, and political activity.

Finally, we must be willing to pay the price.

The challenges we face in helping handicapped newborns grow up to find acceptance and meaningful roles in American society are sizeable. We deceive ourselves if we do not acknowledge from the outset that overcoming those challenges will be costly.

The costs fall most directly on the disabled child's family: financial burdens, emotional stress, relationship strains between parents and among siblings, worry about the future. If we are to put a stop to infanticide, we as a society must be ready to help families meet these costs. We must be willing to pay the price, not only in dollars but also in time, energy, and compassion.

There will be times when, even with the best help society can offer, a family will simply be incapable of shouldering the burdens involved in raising a handicapped child. As we have seen, there are other families who stand ready to adopt these children, to give them a home, and a family, and a future. Surely the answer is to facilitate such adoptions, not—as often happens—to simply let the child die.

The testimony of families who *have* met the challenge of raising a handicapped child is that the rewards far outweigh the costs. It is vitally important to keep this in mind when counseling parents of a disabled newborn in the midst of their confusion and fear. Just as the choices we make as individuals either ennoble or degrade us as moral beings, so the ideals to which we call one another either ennoble or degrade us as a society. We do families, and ourselves, a grave disservice by counselling cynicism rather than hope, fear rather than courage.

We *can* put a stop to infanticide. The time to begin is now. It has been said that the test of a good society is how it cares for those who cannot care for themselves. Our society stands in danger of failing that test. Infanticide may prove to be the issue on which the civility of our civilization stands or falls. The first domino, abortion, fell with a resounding crash. The second domino, infanticide, presently hangs in the balance. We can stop it if we are willing to pay the price. Can we afford not to?

Sources of Information

Disability Rights Groups

Association for Retarded Citizens
2501 Avenue J
Arlington, Texas 76001

The Association for the Severely Handicapped
7010 Roosevelt Way N.E.
Seattle, Washington 98115

Disability Rights Center
1346 Connecticut Ave. N.W.
Washington, D.C. 20036

Down's Syndrome Congress
1640 W. Roosevelt Road
Chicago, Illinois 60608

Spina Bifida Association of America
343 S. Dearborn St.
Chicago, Illinois 60604

Adoption Advocates

Aid to Adoption of Special Kids
411 Wildwood Ave.

Piedmont, California 94611

National Committee for Adoption
1346 Connecticut Ave. N.W.
Washington, D.C. 20036

Prolife Organizations

American Life Lobby
P.O. Box 490
Stafford, Virginia 22554

Americans United for Life
230 N. Michigan Avenue
Chicago, Illinois 60601

Christian Action Council
422 C Street N.E.
Washington, D.C. 20002

National Right to Life Committee
419 7th Street N.W.
Washington, D.C. 20004.

Notes

Chapter One
The Untold Story of Infant Doe

1. Chicago *Tribune,* April 18, 1983, p. 1.
2. "Declatory Judgment in the Matter of the Treatment and Care of Infant Doe," Judge John G. Baker, Monroe County Circuit Court (April 12, 1982).
3. Transcript of April 13, 1982, in regards to Infant Doe, a child in need of services, No. JU-8204-038A (Circuit Court of Monroe County, Indiana).
4. Dr. James Laughlin, quoted in Bloomington *Herald-Telephone*, April 15, 1982; Dr. Ann Bannon, "The Case of the Bloomington Baby," *Human Life Review* (Fall 1982), pp. 63-68.
5. Quoted by Nat Hentoff, *Village Voice,* December 19, 1983.
6. Bloomington *Herald-Telephone,* April 14, 1983.
7. "Declaratory Judgment."
8. Steven R. Valentine, *Heartbeat* (Summer 1983), p. 16.
9. *Indianapolis Star,* May 19, 1982.
10. James Bopp, Jr., "The Legal Implications of Medical Procedures Affecting the Born," in *Human Life and Health Care Ethics.* James Bopp, Jr., ed. (Frederick, Maryland: University Publications of America. In press).
11. *Human Life Review* (Fall 1982), p. 68.
12. Bloomington *Herald-Telephone,* April 16, 1982.
13. *Lifeletter,* '82 #6, p. 4, quoting *Catholic New York* (April 25).
14. Bloomington *Herald-Telephone,* April 16, 1982.
15. Bloomington *Herald-Telephone,* April 19, 1982.

Chapter Two
The Secret Crime

1. Chicago *Tribune,* June 30, 1983, and July 7, 1983.
2. Hartford *Courant,* June 17, 1981.
3. 49 Fed. Reg. 1645, January 12, 1984.
4. Raymond S. Duff and A.G.M. Campbell, "Moral and Ethical Dilemmas in the Special-Care Nursery, *New England Journal of Medicine,* vol. 289 (1973), pp: 890-894.

5. *New England Journal of Medicine,* vol. 290 (1974), p. 518.
6. James Gustafson, "Mongolism, Parental Desires, and the Right to Life," *Perspectives in Biology and Medicine* (Summer 1973), p. 529.
7. Hartford *Courant,* June 14, 1981.
8. 49 Fed. Reg. 1629.
9. See George J. Annas, "Denying the Rights of the Retarded: The Phillip Becker Case, *Hastings Center Report,* December 1979, pp. 18-20; George F. Will, "The Case of Phillip Becker," *Newsweek,* April 14, 1980, and "A Trip Toward Death," *Newsweek,* August 31, 1981; and Gerard E. Sherry, "Phillip Becker: A Life Worth Saving," *Our Sunday Visitor,* November 27, 1983.
10. See Chapter 8.
11. Hartford *Courant,* June 14, 1981.
12. Milton Heifetz, *The Right to Die* (New York: Putnam's, 1975), p. 45.
13. For a discussion of the Edelin case, see John T. Noonan, Jr., *A Private Choice* (New York: The Free Press, 1979), pp. 128-136.
14. Vital Statistics of the United States, 1978, vol. II—Mortality, Part A; Public Health Service, National Center for Health Statistics.
15. Statement of George Little, "Hearings before the Subcommittee on Family and Human Services of the Committee on Labor and Human Resources, U.S. Senate, April 6, 1983 (Washington, D.C.: Government Printing Office), p. 57.
16. Quoted by Nat Hentoff, *Village Voice,* December 19, 1983.
17. Bloomington *Herald-Telephone,* April 16, 1982.
18. Associated Press Report, *Ann Arbor News,* April 17, 1983.
19. These complaints are summarized in the *Federal Register,* pp. 1646-1649.
20. New York *Times,* April 7, 1983.
21. Birth Defects Branch, Center for Environmental Health. Center for Disease Control. Atlanta.
22. Roberta Christianson, et. al. "Incidence of Congenital Anomalies among White and Black Live Births with Long-Term Follow-Up," *American Journal of Public Health,* vol. 71, no. 12 (1981), pp. 1333-1341.

Chapter Three
To Cure or To Kill?

1. Anthony Shaw, "Doctor, Do We Have a Choice?" *New York Times Magazine* (January 30, 1972), pp. 44-54.
2. Anthony Shaw, "Dilemmas of 'Informed Consent' in Children," New England Journal of Medicine, vol. 289, no. 17 (October 25, 1973), pp. 885-890.
3. Anthony Shaw, et al., "Ethical Issues in Pediatric Surgery: A National Survey of Pediatrician and Pediatric Surgeons," *Pediatrics,* vol. 60, no. 4, Part 2 (October 1977), pp. 588-599.
4. I. David Todres, et. al., "Pediatricians' Attitudes Affecting Decision-Making in Defective Newborns," *Pediatrics,* vol. 60 (1977), pp. 197-201.

5. "Treating the Defective Newborn: A Survey of Physicians' Attitudes," *Hastings Center Report* (April 1976), p. 2.

6. Raymond S. Duff, "Counseling Families and Deciding Care of Severely Defective Children: A Way of Coping with 'Medical Vietnam.'" *Pediatrics*, vol. 67 (1981), pp. 315-320.

7. Raymond S. Duff and A.G.M. Campbell, "Moral and Ethical Dilemmas in the Special Care Nursery," *New England Journal of Medicine*, vol. 289 (1973).

8. Transcript, *People ex rel. Washburn v. Stony Brook Hospital*, No. 83-19910 (N.Y. Sup. Ct. Oct. 19, 1983).

9. John Lorber, "Results of Treatment of Myelomeningocele," *Development: Medical Child Neurology*, vol. 13 (1971), pp. 279-303; Early Results of Selective Treatment of Spinal Bifida Cyctica," *British Medical Journal*, vol. 27 (October 1973), pp. 201-204.

10. C. Everett Koop, "Ethical and Surgical Considerations in the Care of the Newborn with Congenital Abnormalities," in Dennis J. Horan and Melinda Delahoyde, eds., *Infanticide and the Handicapped Newborn* (Provo, Utah: Brigham Young University Press, 1982), pp. 89-106.

11. R.B. Zachary, "Life with Spina Bifida," *British Medical Journal*, vol. 2 (1977), pp. 1460-1462.

12. Ibid.

13. John Lorber, "Elective Treatment of Myelomeningocele: To Treat or Not to Treat?" *Pediatrics*, vol. 53, no. 3 (March 1974), pp. 307-308.

14. Milton Heifetz, *The Right to Die* (New York: Putnam's, 1975), p. 59.

15. "Death in the Nursery," documentary by WNEV-TV, Boston, April 1983.

16. See Chapter 9.

17. "Death in the Nursery."

18. Ibid.

19. "Ethical Issues in Pediatric Surgery," p. 592.

20. "Pediatricians' Attitudes Affecting Decision-Making in Defective Newborns," p. 199.

21. John M. Freeman, "To Treat or Not to Treat: Ethical Dilemmas of Treating the Infant with a Myelomeningocele," *Clinical Neurosurgery*, vol. 20 (1973), pp. 143, 144.

22. *American Medical News*, December 11, 1981.

Chapter Four
Doctors and Decisions

1. Milton Heifetz, *The Right to Die* (New York: Putnam's, 1975) pp. 55-56, 69.

2. *Deciding to Forego Life-Sustaining Treatment*, report of President's Commission for the Study of Ethical Problems in Medicine and Biomedical and Behavioral Research, March 1983, pp. 214-215.

3. Diana Crane, *The Sanctity of Social Life: Physicians' Treatment of Critically Ill Patients* (New York: Russell Sage Foundation, 1975), p. 76.

4. Raymond S. Duff, "Guidelines for Deciding Care of Critically Ill or Dying Patients," *Pediatrics,* vol. 64, no. 1 (July 1979), pp. 21-22.
5. Statement of Raymond S. Duff, "Hearings before the Subcommittee on Select Education of the Committee on Education and Labor," House of Representatives, Sept 16, 1982 (Washington, D.C.: Government Printing Office), p. 22.
6. Raymond S. Duff, "Counseling Families and Deciding Care of Severely Defective Children: A Way of Coping with 'Medical Vietnam,' *Pediatrics,* vol. 67 (1981), p. 318.
7. Statement of Raymond S. Duff, Hearing before Subcommittee on Select Education, p. 19.
8. "Guidelines for Deciding," p. 20.
9. "Counseling Families," p. 318.
10. "Death in the Nursery," documentary by WNEV-TV, Boston, April 1983.
11. Hartford *Courant,* June 14, 1981.
12. Anthony Shaw, et. al., "Ethical Issues in Pediatric Surgery: A National Survey of Pediatricians and Pediatric Surgeons," *Pediatrics,* vol. 60, no. 4, Part 2 (October 1977), p. 592.
13. Norman Fost, "Counseling Families Who Have a Child with a Severe Congenital Anomaly," *Pediatrics,* vol. 67, no. 3 (March 1981), pp. 321-324.
14. Rosalyn Darling, "Parents, Physicians, and Spina Bifida," *Hastings Center Report* (August 1977), pp. 10-14.

Chapter Five
Birth, Death, and the Quality of Life

1. Joseph Fletcher, "Indicators of Humanhood: A Tentative Profile of Man, *Hastings Center Report* (November 1972), p. 3.
2. Peter Singer, "Sanctity of Life or Quality of Life?" *Pediatrics,* vol. 72, no. 1 (July 1983), pp. 128-129.
3. Glanville Williams, *The Sanctity of Life and the Criminal Law* (New York: Knopf, 1957). Quoted in James T. Burtchaell, *Rachel Weeping* (Kansas City: Andrews and McMeel, 1982), p. 296.
4. Michael Tooley, "Abortion and Infanticide," *Philosophy and Public Affairs,* vol. 2, no. 1 (1972), pp. 37-65.
5. Tristram Englehardt, "Ethical Issues in Aiding the Death of Small Children," in Marvin Kohl, ed., *Beneficent Euthanasia* (Buffalo: Prometheus Books, 1975), p. 184.
6. Joseph Fletcher, *Humanhood: Essays in Biomedical Ethics* (Buffalo: Prometheus Books, 1979), p. 147.
7. Richard McCormick, S.J., "To Save or Let Die: the Dilemma of Modern Medicine," *Journal of the American Medical Association,* vol. 229, no. 2 (July 8, 1974), pp. 172-176.
8. See Robert Barry, O.P., "Euthanasia and the Church," *Catholicism in Crisis* (February 1984), pp. 10-12.

9. A.R. Jonson, S.J., et al., "Critical Issues in Newborn Intensive Care: A Conference Report and Policy Proposal," *Pediatrics,* vol. 55, no. 6 (June 1975), pp. 756-768.
10. "A New Medical Ethic," *California Medicine* (September, 1970), pp. 67-68.
11. "Abortion and Infanticide."
12. "Indicators of Humanhood," pp. 1-4.
13. "Ethical Issues," p. 185.
14. Hunter C. Leake, III, et. al., "Active Euthanasia with Parental Consent," *Hastings Center Report* (October 1979), pp. 19-21.
15. Marvin Kohl, "Voluntary Beneficent Euthanasia," in Marvin Kohl, ed., Beneficent Euthanasia (Buffalo: Prometheus, 1975) p. 135.
16. Daniel C. Maguire, "A Catholic View of Mercy Killing," *Beneficent Euthanasia,* p. 36. See also Maguire's *Death by Choice* (New York: Doubleday, 1974).
17. Joseph Fletcher, "Ethics and Euthanasia," in Dennis J. Horan and David Mall, eds., *Death, Dying, and Euthanasia* (Frederick, Maryland: University Publications of America, 1980), p. 301.
18. "Voluntary Beneficent Euthanasia," pp. 133, 134.
19. "Ethical Issues," p. 186.
20. Joseph Fletcher, "The 'Right' To Live and the 'Right' To Die," in *Beneficent Euthanasia,* p. 49.

Chapter Six
Hard Cases and Hard Questions

1. *Current Opinions of the Judicial Council of the American Medical Association, 1981,* Article 2.10.
2. This quote and those following are from Fr. McCormick's paper, "To Save or Let Die: The Dilemma of Modern Medicine,"*Journal of the American Medical Association,* vol. 229, no. 2 (July 8, 1974), pp. 172-176.
3. Richard A. McCormick, "The Quality of Life, the Sanctity of Life," *Hastings Center Report* (February 1978), pp. 30-36.
4. Richard A. McCormick and Lawrence H. Tribe, "Infant Doe: Drawing the Line," *American Medical News* (October 15, 1982).
5. John J. Paris and Richard A. McCormick, "Saving Defective Infants: Options for Life or Death," *America* (April 23, 1983), pp. 313-317.
6. Dennis J. Horan, "Euthanasia as a Form of Medical Management," in *Death, Dying, and Euthanasia,* Dennis J. Horan and David Mall, eds. (Frederick, Maryland: University Publications of America), pp. 196-227.
7. "To Save or Let Die," pp. 172-173.
8. "The Quality of Life, the Sanctity of Life," p. 30.
9. Joseph Fletcher, "The 'Right' To Live and the 'Right' To Die," in Marvin

Kohl, ed., *Beneficent Euthanasia* (Buffalo: Prometheus, 1975), pp. 44-53.

10. Statement of John J. Paris, "Hearings before the Subcommittee on Family and Human Services," U.S. Senate, April 6, 1983, p. 87.

11. John J. Paris, "Terminating Treatment for Newborns: A Theological Perspective," *Law, Medicine and Health Care* (June 1982), pp. 120-124.

12. "The Quality of Life, the Sanctity of Life," p. 174.

13. Paul Ramsey, *Ethics at the Edges of Life* (New Haven: Yale University Press, 1978), p. 156.

14. Quoted in Ramsey, Ibid., p. 256.

15. Fred Lilly, "Defending the Helpless," *National Catholic Register,* August 28, 1983.

16. *To Live in Christ Jesus,* A Pastoral Reflection on the Moral Life, National Conference of Catholic Bishops, November 11, 1976.

17. For a useful discussion of these points see Donald McCarthy and Edward Bayer, eds., *Handbook on Critical Life Issues*, St. Louis: Pope John XXIII Medical-Moral Research and Education Center, 1982), see especially chapter 13, "Decisions About Prolonging Life."

Chapter Seven
From the Delivery Room to the Courtroom

1. John A. Robertson, "Dilemma in Danville," *Hastings Center Report* (October 1981), p. 5.

2. Ibid. However, parents and physicians *have* been prosecuted for killing newborns by active means, as well as for withholding routine care to otherwise healthy newborns.

3. See, for example, T. S. Ellis, III, "Letting Defective Babies Die. Who Decides?" *American Journal of Law and Medicine*, vol. 7, no. 4, p. 402.

4. John A. Robertson, "Legal Aspects of Withholding Medical Treatment from Handicapped Children," in Horan and Delahoyde, eds., *Infanticide and the Handicapped Newborn* (Provo, Utah: Brigham Young University Press, 1982), pp. 89-106.

5. John A. Robertson, "Involuntary Euthanasia of Defective Newborns: A Legal Analysis," in Horan and Mall, eds., *Death, Dying, and Euthanasia*, (Frederick, Maryland: University Publications of America), pp. 196-227.

6. Ibid., p. 156.

7. Ibid., pp. 158-160.

8. James Bopp, "The Legal Implications of Medical Procedures Affecting the Born," James Bopp, Jr., ed, *Human Life and Health Care Ethics* (University Publications).

9. Ibid.

10. Ibid.

11. Ibid.

12. John C. Blattner, "The Silent Holocaust: Step II," *New Covenant*, (September 1983), pp. 17-18.

13. Ibid., p. 18.
14. Rowine Hayes Brown and Richard B. Truitt, "Euthanasia and the Right to Die," *Ohio Northern University Law Review,* vol. 3, no. 3 (1976), pp. 631, 636.
15. Robertson, "Involuntary Euthanasia," p. 169.
16. "Death in the Nursery," documentary by WNEV-TV, Boston, April 1983.
17. "Legal Implications," p. 32.
18. Los Angeles *Times,* January 2, 1984.
19. Ellis, "Letting Defective Babies Die," pp. 415-416.
20. "Dilemma in Danville," p. 7.
21. "Legal Aspects," p. 24.
22. "Involuntary Euthanasia," p. 194.

Chapter Eight
In the Matter of Baby Jane Doe

1. *Newsday,* November 4, 1983; New York *Times,* November 6, 1983; Washington Post, November 16, 1983; Los Angeles *Times*, November 5, 1983.
2. *Newsday*, October 18, 1983; L.A. *Times*, November 5, 1983; Washington *Post*, December 27, 1983.
3. New York *Daily News,* October 21, 1983; N.Y. *Times*, October 21, 1983.
4. *Newsday,* October 22, 1983.
5. *Newsday,* October 23, 1983; N.Y. *Times,* October 25, 1983.
6. N.Y. *Times,* October 29, 1983.
7. Washington *Times,* December 12, 1983.
8. *United States v. University Hospital*, No. 83-6343 (U.S. Ct. of Appeals, 2nd Circ, February 23, 1984), majority opinion; p. 8.
9. Washington *Post,* November 3, 1983.
10. *Newsday*, October 30, 1983; Washington *Post*, November 3, *1983; Newsday,* November 4, 1983; Washington *Post*, November 16, 1983.
11. *Newsday,* November 5, 1983.
12. N.Y. *Times,* November 7, 1983.
13. *Newsday,* November 5, 1983.
14. "60 Minutes," CBS News, March 11, 1984.
15. L.A. *Times,* November 5, 1983.
16. "Face the Nation," CBS News, November 6, 1983.
17. Transcript, *People ex rel. Washburn v. Stony Brook Hospital*, No.83-19910 (N.Y. Sup. Ct. October 19, 1983). Transcript courtesy of Americans United for Life.
18. L.A. *Times,* November 4, 1983.
19. N.Y. *Times,* November 1, 1983; November 4, 1983.
20. *Wall Street Journal*, October 31, 1983.
21. Ann Arbor *News,* November 17, 1983.
22. Washington *Post,* November 13, 1983.

23. "60 Minutes," CBS News, March 11, 1984.
24. *Stony Brook Hospital*, transcript, note 16, *supra*.
25. Telephone interview, November 30, 1983; courtesy Americans United for Life.
26. "60 Minutes," CBS News, March 11, 1984.
27. Statement of David G. McLone, "Hearings before the Subcommittee on Family and Human Services," p. 66.
28. In April, 1984, it was reported that Baby Jane's parents allowed a shunt to be implanted to drain the excess fluid from her brain, and that she went home from the hospital. However, other corrective surgery was not performed and her long-range prospects remain an open question. It was also reported that her given name is Keri-Lynn, though her surname still has not been made public. See *National Right to Life News,* April 19, 1984.

Chapter Nine
Death and Due Process in Oklahoma

1. The story of Carlton Johson was told in a three-part film report, "Who Lives, Who Dies?" broadcast on the Cable News Network, February 21-23, 1984. The reporter who produced the series was Pulitzer-Prize winning journalist Carlton Sherwood, now with the Washington *Times*.
2. Sherwood had a signed affidavit from Mrs. Johnson authorizing access to her son's records.
3. "Comments of the American Academy of Pediatrics on Proposed Rule," July 5, 1983, pp. 50-51.
4. Richard H. Gross, M.D., et al., "Early Management and Decision Making for the Treatment of Myelomeningocele," *Pediatrics,* vol. 72, no. 4 (October 1983), pp. 450-458.
5. "Who Lives, Who Dies?"
6. Ibid.
7. Ibid.
8. Ibid.
9. Ibid.
10. Ibid.
11. *Deciding to Forego Life-Sustaining Treatment,* report of President's Commission for the Study of Ethical Problems in Medicine and Biomedical and Behavioral Research, March 1983, note 106, pp. 155-156.
12. Bernard N. Nathanson, *Aborting America* (Toronto: Life Cycle Books, 1979), pp. 39-41.
13. *In re: Karen Quinlan,* 137 N.J. Super. 227 (1975), reprinted Dennis Horan and David Mall, eds., *Death, Dying, and Euthanasia* (University Publications of America, 1980), pp. 510-511.
14. "Who Lives, Who Dies?"
15. The letter, dated February 24, 1984, was signed by Dee Everitt, president of the Association for Retarded Citizens; Kent Smith,

executive director of the Spina Bifida Association of America; Wayne Sailor, president of The Association for Persons with Severe Handicaps (TASH); Thomas O'Neill, president of the Down's Syndrome Congress; Nat Hentoff, author; and Martin Gerry, former director of the Office for Civil Rights of the Department of Health, Education, and Welfare.

16. "Who Lives, Who Dies?"
17. Ibid.

Chapter Ten
Of Dominoes and Slippery Slopes

1. Paul Ramsey, Introduction to Horan and Delahoyde, eds., *Infanticide and the Handicapped Newborn* (Provo, Utah: Brigham Young University Press, 1982), p. xiv.
2. *Korematsu v. U.S.*, 323 U.S. 214 (1944).
3. *Infanticide and the Handicapped Newborn*, pp. xiii-xiv.
4. Quoted in John Powell, *Abortion: the Silent Holocaust*, (Allen, Texas: Argus Communications, 1981), p. 44.
5. Ibid.
6. John C. Blattner, "The Silent Holocaust: Step II," *New Covenant* (September 1983), p. 20.
7. *In re: Karen Quinlan*, 137 N.J. Super. 227 (1975). Emphasis added.
8. Charles E. Rice, "Amniocentesis, Coercion, and Privacy," in Leonard J. Nelson, ed., *The Death Decision* (Ann Arbor: Servant Books, 1984), p. 62.
9. Dennis J. Horan and Steven R. Valentine, "The Doctor's Dilemma: Euthanasia, Wrongful Life, and the Handicapped Newborn," in Horan and Delahoyde, eds., *Infanticide and the Handicapped Newborn*, pp. 48-49.
10. Leo Alexander, "Medical Science Under Dictatorship," in Horan and Mall, eds., *Death, Dying, and Euthanasia* (Frederick, Maryland: University Publications, 1980), p. 584.
11. Frederic Wertham, "The Geranium in the Window: the 'Euthanasia' Murders," in Horan and Mall, eds., p. 610.
12. "Medical Science Under Dictatorship," p. 572.
13. Ibid., p. 573.
14. "The Geranium in the Window," p. 630.
15. Peter Singer, "Sanctity of Life or Quality of Life?," *Pediatrics,* vol. 72, no. 1 (July 1983), pp. 128-129.
16. Budetti, et. al., "The Costs and Effectiveness of Neonatal Intensive Care," August 1981, Office of Technology Assessment, Washington, D.C., p. 40.
17. "The Silent Holocaust," p. 20.
18. Haynes Johnson, Washington *Post,* April 3, 1984.
19. New York *Times,* April 12, 1984.
20. Quoted in David W. Louisell, "Euthanasia and Biathanasia: On Dying and Killing," in *Death, Dying, and Euthanasia,* p. 389.

21. Yale Kamisar, "Some Non-Religious Views Against Proposed 'Mercy-Killing' Legislation," in *Death, Dying, and Euthanasia*, p. 473-474.
22. "Medical Science under Dictatorship," p. 587.

Chapter Eleven
Rights, Regulations, and the Role of Government

1. The President's memo to Attorney General Smith and Secretary Schweicker was dated April 30, 1982. On May 18, 1982, the director of HHS's Office for Civil Rights, Betty Lou Dotson, sent a notice to some 6,400 hospitals and other health care institutions reminding them of the applicability of Section 504 to the care of handicapped newborns.
2. 48 Fed. Reg. 9630, March 7, 1983.
3. *American Academy of Pediatrics v. Heckler*, 561 F. Supp. 395 (D.D.C. 1983). The opinion was announced April 14, 1983.
4. The proposed legislation was first introduced as a separate bill on May 26, 1982, as H.R. 6492. In 1983 it was revamped and added as a proposed amendment to H.R. 1904, a bill to renew the Child Abuse Prevention and Treatment Act and the Child Abuse Prevention and Treatment and Adoption Reform Act of 1978.
5. S. 1003, introduced April 7, 1983.
6. Proposed revised regulations were published July 5, 1983, marking the beginning of a 60-day public comment period. 48 Fed. Reg. 30846.
7. This statement is discussed more fully in Chapter 12.
8. 49 Fed. Reg. 1622, January 12, 1984.
9. The suit was filed March 12, 1984, in the U.S. District Court for Southern New York, by the American Medical Association, the American Academy of Family Physicians, the Association of American Medical Colleges, the American College of Obstetricians and Gynecologists, the American Hospital Association, the Hospital Association of New York State, and a group of individual physicians.
10. The decision was announced May 24, 1984.
11. H.R. 1904, passed February 3, 1984.

Chapter Twelve
Changing Doctors' Minds

1. Francis A. Schaeffer and C. Everett Koop, *Whatever Happened to the Human Race?* (Old Tappan, N.J.: Fleming Revell, 1979), p. 74.
2. Koop, "Ethical and Surgical Considerations in the Care of the Newborn with Congenital Abnormalities," in Dennis Horan and Melinda Delahoyde, eds., *Infanticide and the Handicapped Newborn* (Provo, Utah: Brigham Young University Press, 1982), pp. 89-106.
3. Ibid., p. 100.
4. John C. Blattner, "The Silent Holocaust: Step II," *New Covenant* (September 1983), p. 19.
5. Ibid.
6. "Ethical and Surgical Considerations," p. 99.

7. C. Everett Koop, "The Silent Domino: Infanticide," *Congressional Record,* Tuesday, July 17, 1979, p. 140.
8. *Whatever Happened to the Human Race?,* p. 56.
9. "Moral and Ethical Dilemmas," p. 898.
10. *Whatever Happened to the Human Race?,* p. 74.
11. Raymond S. Duff and A.G.M. Campbell, "Moral and Ethical Dilemmas in the Special Care Nursery," *New England Journal of Medicine,* vol. 289 (1973), pp. 890-894.
12. *Whatever Happened to the Human Race?,* p. 74.
13. "Moral and Ethical Dilemmas," p. 894.
14. *Whatever Happened to the Human Race?,* p. 74.
15. Anthony Shaw, "Dilemmas of Informed Consent in Children," *New* England Journal of Medicine, vol. 289, no. 17 (October 25, 1973), pp. 885-890.
16. *Whatever Happened to the Human Race?,* p. 68.
17. The article on this subject most frequently reprinted in medical texts is Fr. McCormick's "To Save or Let Die." See, for example, *Biomedical Ethics,* Thomas Mappes and Jane Zembaty, eds. (New York: McGraw-Hill, 1981); *Bioethics,* Thomas A. Shannon, ed. (Ramsey, New Jersey: Paulist Press, 1981); *Ethics in Medicine,* Stanley Reiser, et al. eds. (Cambridge, Massachusetts: The MIT Press, 1977).
18. *Mental Retardation: The Leading Edge,* Staff Report of the President's Committee on Mental Retardation (Washington, D.C.: U.S. Government Printing Office, 1979), Publication No. 79-21018, pp. 3-5.
19. 49 Fed. Reg. 1629, January 12, 1984.

Chapter Thirteen
The End of the Mythical American

1. Frank Bowe, *Handicapping America: Barriers to Disabled People* (New York: Harper and Row, 1978), pp. 16-28.
2. Ibid, p. 135.
3. From J. Turem, ed. *Report of the Comprehensive Service Needs Study.* Washington, D.C.: The Urban Institute, 1975. Quoted in Bowe, *Handicapping America,* pp. 220-223.
4. *Handicapping America,* p. 164.
5. *Mental Retardation: The Leading Edge,* pp. 45-46; Robert Perske, *New Life in the Neighborhood* (Nashville: Abingdon, 1980), p. 68.
6. *Handicapping America,* p. 181.
7. *New Life in the Neighborhood,* p. 33.
8. *Buck v. Bell,* 274 U.S. 200 (1927).
9. *Disability Rag,* May 1983.

Chapter Fourteen
Whose Life Is Worth Living?

1. *Newsweek* (November 12, 1973).
2. Sondra Diamond, "On Being Alive," *Human Life Review* (Fall 1977).

3. Francis A. Schaeffer and C. Everett Koop, *Whatever Happened to the Human Race?* (Old Tappan, New Jersey: Fleming Revell, 1979), p. 65.
4. Frank Bowe, *Comeback* (New York: Harper and Row, 1981), p. 114.
5. *Whatever Happened to the Human Race?*, pp. 64-65.
6. Testimony of Carl and Rachel Rossow before the Subcommittee on Family and Human Services, pp. 122-131.
7. No one knows how many American children are in foster care. Estimates ranged from 350,000 to 750,000 in testimony before the Senate Subcommittee on Family and Human Services in April 1983. The high estimate of 750,000 was made by Laurie Flynn, director of the North American Council on Adoptable Children. Ibid., p. 558.
8. Ibid., pp. 479, 585.
9. Ibid., p. 481.
10. Ibid., p. 573.
11. Ibid., pp. 571-572.
12. For a comprehensive discussion of impediments to adoption, see Senate pp. 477-570.
13. Ibid., pp. 506-507.
14. "Who Lives, Who Dies?," the Cable News Network, February 21-23, 1984.

Index

Pro-Life Books from Servant

The Zero People
Edited by Jeff Henseley

John T. Noonan, John Powell, Dr. C. Everett Koop, Malcolm Muggeridge, Harold O.J. Brown, George F. Will, and nineteen other distinguished authors, social-critics, and pro-life leaders team up to make this the most up-to-date, indepth, and authoritative single volume treatment available about the assault on life through abortion, infanticide, and euthanasia. $7.95

Justice for the Unborn
Why We Have "Legal" Abortion and How We Can Stop It
Randall J. Hekman

The true story of a judge who fought for the life of an unborn child—and won. $5.95

> "Judge Randall Hekman is a courageous public servant whose new book, Justice for the Unborn, deserves the thoughtful attention of anyone interested in the ultimate civil right." —Congressman Henry Hyde

Available at your Christian bookstore or from
Servant Publications, Dept. 209
P.O. Box 8617, Ann Arbor, MI 48107
Send for your FREE catalog of Christian books, music, and cassettes.